Love Herself

shell.chelle

Love Herself
shell.chelle

Copyright © 2024 shell.chelle
Love Herself

ISBN: 979-8-9912545-2-6

Book & Cover Design: Integrative Ink
www.integrativeink.com

Poetry about a girl.
Just a girl,
Living her life.
Writing down her dreams.
Just a girl.
Imperfect and flawed.
Found her love,
Inside of herself.
Writing some words.
Words that became poetry.

These words became a story.
Her Story.
A story of a girl who:

Lost Herself

Found Herself

Then learned to...

Love Herself

This little side note:

This is her experience.
Her point of view.
Her feelings.
Her perspective.
Her story of letting go.
Her story of leaving,
A world of black and white.
Leaving the darkness,
And finding her light.
Her story of arriving,
To where the grey area resides.
This place of surrender.
This place of light.
A story of her memory.
A story of her truth.
A story from her eyes.
A story from her heart.
A story from her mind.
A story that she remembers,
As she listened to herself.
As she listened on her path.
Her path to self-love.
Her path to self-worth.
Her path to authenticity.
Her path to alignment.
Her path to her soul.
Her path.
Her love.
This is her story.

Also, this.
(In very fine print.)

These words.
These are just words.
Words of poetry.
Poetry to read.
These are just words.
Beautiful words.
Words of poetry.

Love Herself

A Letter Of Love, Signed By Me

A letter.
This letter.
A letter of love.
A letter of power.
A letter of release.
A letter of light.
This letter to myself.
This beautiful me.
This letter of power.
This empowerment to myself.
This letter of release.
This healing.
This letter of light.
The end of the darkness.
This letter is not just a letter.
It is a letter of love.
Signed by me.
But not that same old me,
That everyone knows.
It is signed by a new girl,
That they need to get to know.
Signed by me.
The new me,
That I know.
This new me,
After an awakening.
This new me,
That I made, by myself.
With the love and support...
Of beautiful people,

Cheering me on.
This new me,
That I made,
From the darkness.
This new me,
Rising above.
The storms, the fires,
And the challenges.
This new me,
Had to leave a world.
The only world,
I ever knew.
A world, that I never fit into,
In the first place.
My destiny was,
To create a new world.
Create a new world,
That was fit for me.
This new me,
Created this new world.
My own little world,
My own little creation.
This new world,
Welcomed me.
Welcomed me,
And my light.
This light has been there,
All along.
I just had to move through,
All the layers.
The layers were there,
To be discovered.

This letter is written,
From this new world.
It is written,
After this discovery...
And through all the layers.
It is written,
With clarity and intention.
Openness and love.
Power and strength.
It is written,
With wisdom and honesty.
Naked and truth.
It is written,
With feeling and emotion.
It is written,
With many tears.
It is written,
With my new bravery,
That I found.
This letter.
This letter of love.
Is signed by me.

Love Herself

She will love herself,
No matter what.
She will choose herself,
No matter what.
She will give herself love,
Over and over.
Over and over,
Again and again.
She finally believes...
That she is worthy.
Worthy of love.
This love that she has found for herself.
She finally believes...
She deserves the best.
She finally sees.
Sees herself clearly.
She knows she is worthy.
She knows what she has to give.
She has so much to offer.
She has so much love to give.
She never deserved mistreatment.
She didn't deserve any of it.
She needed to work through,
All the layers.
She needed to find her light,
That was waiting inside.
She needed to discover.
Discover her love.
She needed to pick up all of the pieces.
These pieces she picked up.

Every single piece,
She will cherish.
She will look in the mirror,
And believe she was the one.
She was the one,
All along.
The one that she needed.
The one that she loved.
Her light was found,
Underneath the pain.
Underneath this illusion.
This illusion she held onto.
She held onto it...
So, so tight.
So tightly,
She gripped.
She gripped to this illusion.
Let it all go.
Remove it all.
Let everything go,
Except for her love.
She will keep her love.
She will hold onto this.
She has found her freedom,
As she opened her heart.
She now...
Truly loves herself.

Love For Herself

Who was she before the pain?
Who was she before the hurt?
Who was she before she found her worth?
This little girl loved to write.
She loved to read books,
And stories too.
She loved to be outside,
She loved the sunshine.
Being on the water,
Brought her pure joy.
Being out in nature,
Filled up her heart.
Being active and moving,
Put a smile on her face.
She loved to dance,
And just be free.
What happened to that girl?
Where did she go?
She was covered in pain.
Her shadow self,
Started to lead.
There were events,
That led to loss of her worth.
She lost herself,
She lost her soul.
She had to dig, really deep.
To find her spirit,
It never left.
The pain.
The trauma.

The betrayal.
And illusion.
It all kept her,
From her own soul.
Her light was buried,
Underneath a façade.
A façade that she thought,
Was her true self.
Trauma responses,
Coping And defense mechanisms...
And a heart, that she closed off.
She didn't believe in herself,
At all.
She lost her value.
She lost her worth.
She looked around.
At everyone else,
To love her.
Not knowing it would be found,
Inside of her heart.
She kept her truth to herself.
Hiding underneath fear,
And keeping herself small.
Pleasing everyone else,
Became the norm.
Not feeling her pain,
Became her way.
Running from her hurt,
And shoving her pain aside.
All she wanted was happiness...
She was searching to find it.
Finding it in all the wrong places.

She was looking everywhere,
Instead of herself.
She would finally realize,
The love she was needing.
It was all inside.
Her worth.
Her light.
Her soul.
It never left.
It was all there waiting.
Waiting for her.
Waiting for her to collect tools,
To feel all the pain.
The pain was really deep.
It was extremely hard to face.
But she had the strength now,
To not run away.
She learned to listen.
She learned to stay.
She learned her worth,
It was up to her.
She would believe in herself.
She would value herself.
She would love her heart.
She would stop giving all of this away.
She would keep digging...
Until her light would shine through,
For her to see.
As she found her light,
She would let go of everything else.
And hold onto this,
It was love for herself.

This Is You Now

Stop living for others.
Stop living to please.
Stop living to make people feel comfortable.
Stop living for everyone,
Other than yourself.
It is up to you,
To make your life.
Your life can be anything,
That you choose.
It doesn't matter,
What others say.
All that matters,
Is that you are happy.
All that matters,
Is your heart is open.
All that matters,
Is you set yourself free.
Free from expectations.
Free from rejection.
Free from control.
Free from judgement.
Stop expecting anything of yourself.
Stop rejecting yourself.
Stop controlling yourself.
Stop judging yourself.
Release all of this,
Get rid of it, now.
As soon as you start loving yourself,
You set yourself up...
To be completely free.

Empty out,
Let out the emotions.
Let them out,
No matter how hard it is.
Cry and scream,
Whatever you need.
It will be hard,
Listen to yourself.
Tell yourself,
You are worthy.
You are safe.
Release this darkness.
Release this pain.
Release the expectations.
These expectations of yourself.
Just Release it.
You don't need it.
Let it all go.
Live for yourself.
Live for you.
No more sacrificing.
You are done with that.
Let them talk.
Let them watch.
Let them judge.
You are not living for them.
Not anymore.
Those days are done.
You're living for you.
You're living for love.
Part of love,
Is freedom to choose.

Choose for yourself,
Whatever you need.
Choose for yourself,
Whatever comes,
And whatever goes.
Choose for yourself,
What makes you happy.
What lights you up.
What brings you joy.
This is what you'll choose.
This is where you are going.
This is what you will live for.
You are living for you now,
You're not living for them.
You are no longer a people pleaser.
You no longer will be used.
You are free to respond,
However, you choose.
You are free to go,
Wherever you want to go.
You are free to say,
Whatever it is, that needs to be said.
You are free to set a boundary.
You are free to say no.
You are free to not go.
You are free to disappear,
If that's what you choose.
This life is yours now.
Take control.
Lead with your heart.
Trust that inner guidance.
Your soul will speak.

It's time for you now.
It's time for your soul now.
You are uncovering it.
This is you now.
Release it all.
The burdens are gone now,
You can breathe.
Breathe in.
And
Breathe out.
This is you now.

Soul Self

To be who you really are,
You have to lose.
Lose it all.
Lose yourself.
Lose yourself,
To find your true self.
Lose your old self,
To find your soul self.
Be vulnerable with yourself.
That's where it begins.
See all sides.
Meet all the versions.
Dig deep.
Prepare.
Emotions, you're not equipped to feel.
They are deep down.
Deep down, in there.
Deep down,
Deep within.
Pull it all out.
Get to know it all.
Then release it all.
Let it all go.
Oh, that power.
The power.
That is inside of you.
Each barrier.
Each barrier, there for you to see.
For you to know.
For you to feel.

Release it again.
And again.
And again.
This healing journey.
This healing, I've found.
I'm not who I used to be.
This transition.
This transformation.
Who am I now?
I'm not where I want to be,
But I can feel my soul.
Oh, I can feel it.
I'm getting so close.
My soul self,
That's my goal.
How did I live so long,
Covering it up?
My soul self,
It's who I am.
It's who I've always been.
It's who I was always meant to be.
I'm not living,
Under anyone's expectations.
Expectations of me.
Not anymore.
I'm not living,
For anyone else,
Other than myself.
I should be this.
I should be that.
This is how it's supposed to look.
This is how it's supposed to be.

You're supposed to make this much.
You're supposed to smile,
And always be nice.
Don't upset them.
Walk on eggshells.
Do things you don't want to do.
All to be nice.
All for the show.
I'm done with this.
It feels so shallow.
This is my life.
I get to choose.
I want to live rich.
Rich, as in happiness.
Rich, as in love.
Rich, as in connection.
Rich, as in passion.
Rich, as in fulfillment.
I want to have my own beliefs.
I want to find my soul.
That is my goal.
I will listen.
I will become.
I will be who I was always meant to be.
Not what society wants.
Not what my environment wants.
Not what most people want.
I will exclude myself.
Exclude myself, into my soul.
Exclude myself, to where I need to go.
I will be an outcast.
It's okay.

I will live for me.
I will live for my soul.
My goal is,
To find my soul self.

Free

Free yourself.
Free your mind.
Free your heart.
Free your soul.
Free yourself from anything,
That is not you.
Free yourself from anything,
That doesn't inspire you.
Free yourself from anything,
That requires you to be,
Someone else.
Those expectations.
Those requirements.
Those rules and regulations.
That is not life.
To put on a façade.
That is not life.
To become small.
That just is not life.
I want to feel inspired.
I want my dreams to come true.
I want passion and fulfillment.
I just want to be free.
Freedom comes with chaos.
Freedom is not what's "normal".
Because freedom is not what is taught.
The chaos comes,
From within you.
Grieving, all that was.
The chaos comes,

From everyone else.
The opinions and feelings,
Of those you love.
No, don't change.
No, that's not in the plan.
No, that's not how you should act.
No, that's not safe.
People will see you.
People will judge.
What will people think?
Do you know what freedom taught me?
None of that matters.
Because, once you have complete,
Trust in yourself...
It is you that becomes,
The one who matters.
The outer world becomes so vague.
The opinions become a blur.
The judgment becomes a whisper,
That you no longer can hear.
Because all you can see,
Is what is for you.
What is in front of you.
Your calling.
Your destiny.
An opinion,
And judgement can't take that away.
Let them talk,
I will not stay.
What is right for everyone else,
Is not what's right for me.
Society's way,

Is not my way.
My way...
Is grieving all that I was,
And letting myself be free.
Free from it all.
Free from those expectations.
Free from all that I knew.
And becoming true,
To what has always been,
Inside of me.
I will be true,
To me.

On my own

I'm on my own.
If I fall on my face,
It's me,
That picks myself back up.
If I get burned,
I mend myself back together again.
Betray me,
I nurture myself back to health.
Leave me,
Don't worry...
I've got my own back.
I'm on my own.
It's me, that's here.
You're afraid of hurting me?
Oh,
I'm a big girl.
You can't hurt me,
Like I've been hurt before.
Never again,
Can I be kicked down.
Never again...
Will I be bruised,
Like I have in the past.
I am on my own.
Because I've been on my own,
I know how to mend, all of my wounds.
My heart has been broken,
Many times.
It is me that's held it,
So that it can heal.

I'm on my own.
I've given my heart,
To people who didn't know how to handle it.
Now I realize,
It's me.
I'm the one who knows how to handle it.
I can hold my heart,
Along with someone else.
I've learned to share my love,
Not give it all away.
Pour it all out.
Pour it into the takers.
Pour it into the people,
Who walk away.
Pour it into the people,
Who don't have love for themselves.
Pour it into the people,
Who see my love,
And take it for them.
I now know how to share.
I have learned to give,
Without pouring it all out,
In just one shot.
I've learned that it's me,
That becomes empty.
And they leave,
Filled up.
Filled up with my love.
That was before,
I knew my worth.
That was before,
I believed I deserved all of my love.

I can decide who to share it with.
I'm on my own.
At the end of the day,
Who do I have?
It's me.
It's me that will take care of me.
It's me that will need, all of that love.
It's me what will appreciate me.
I'm on my own.
It's a beautiful thing.
It is beautiful to find love for yourself.
It is beautiful to be on my own.

Tears Of Love

Grieving all of the girls that I used to be.
Grieving all of them.
I mourn for them.
All of these girls,
Had so much love.
Love for people,
I had to let go of.
Grief for a life,
That won't proceed.
Grief for a life,
I painted for me.
Loss of people.
Loss of myself.
Loss of this girl,
I once was.
Parts of me,
I will have to let go.
These tears are for them.
These tears are love.
Streaming from my eyes.
These tears of love,
Leaving my soul.
This is what grief feels like,
To me.
These tears of love,
Leaving my body.
These tears in my eyes.
These tears of pain.
Each time I grieve,
I become someone new.

Grieving who I was,
Who I used to be.
Grieving this loss,
More tears will come.
This grief,
I will carry with me.
This grief,
Fills me up inside.
I carry this pain.
I let it go with tears.
These tears are just love.
Love that I had.
Love.
I have to let go of.
Let go.
To make room for more love.
Release this love.
Release these tears.
Release this pain.
Hope will come again.
This release of grief,
Makes space for hope.
This release of grief,
Makes room for love.
Cry these tears.
Face this darkness.
Light will come again.
This process of grief,
Must be acknowledged.
I acknowledge you.
I see you.
Grief needs to be seen.
Don't run away.

Sit with my grief.
Hold it close.
It's not here to stay.
It is just a wave.
A wave,
Coming upon me.
Here it is now,
It will soon leave.
These tears.
So many.
My heart aches.
It feels like my heart will beat,
Right out of my chest.
I acknowledge this pain.
I will sit with it.
I will feel it.
My heart,
It feels,
Ripped open.
A tear.
This tear.
It feels so raw.
I will mend my heart,
With these tears.
These tears of love.
Let them leave.
These tears of love.
Flow out of me.
These tears of love.
These tears of grief.
I mourn for you.
I mourn for me.

This Light

We live in a world,
Of instant gratification.
We live in a world,
Of judgment and opinions.
We live in a world of emotional suppression.
We live in a world of speed and succession.
How fast can you go?
How fast can you succeed?
Competition and entitlement.
The need to be right.
The need to win.
Your achievements and your job.
You are what you do.
Doing over feeling.
Rushing over rest.
Living with plans versus living in the moment.
I am living in this world,
Feeling all alone.
It is just me.
Am I the only one who sees?
I need to find what is in alignment.
Alignment with me.
Alignment with where I am going.
What is in alignment with who I really am.
This healing in me.
This awakening for myself.
These phases of growth.
This shift in vibration.
I have changed my vibration.
I am vibrating in another realm.

This frequency is new.
New to me.
New to feel.
My aura is new.
I see into your aura.
This aura of projection.
Projecting your feelings.
Projection of anger.
Projection of perfection.
Projection of fixing.
Suppress and keep going.
No time for you to feel.
You want to change me.
You don't want to accept me for me.
You want me to come back.
Come back to where you are.
You want me back to my ego self.
My ego, I left.
I don't need it anymore.
Not here.
Not in my new aura.
I will speak my truth.
I will speak my peace.
I will speak only from my authentic place.
I can't go back.
Go back to that.
I need to keep moving.
Moving ahead.
These higher vibrations.
I feel this power.
I feel this magnitude.
I feel alive.

These vibrations.
This higher realm.
This is where I belong.
This is where I must be.
This place of honesty.
This place of staying humble.
This place of authenticity.
This place of love.
This place of enlightenment.
This is what is ahead.
I am feeling inspired,
Through the darkness.
This light,
I see.
This light,
I feel.
This light is love.
Love for me.

Healing The World

Walking away from all that you know.
Walking away,
Following your heart.
Follow your intuition.
Follow your inner guidance.
Listen closely.
Listen to your own voice.
When there is something else,
That is meant for you.
When there is a purpose,
That is waiting for you.
That purpose may not be easy to see.
That purpose may be underneath the layers.
Layers for you to uncover.
Layers of pain.
Layers that are not really you.
That purpose lies inside of you.
It is digging through the layers,
Until it is uncovered.
That purpose is there.
Trust and surrender.
That purpose is yours.
It is all yours.
That purpose is inside.
Let each layer peel away.
Listen and see each layer that is there.
This is finding intimacy with yourself.
This is finding your own vulnerability.
This is inside.
It is all within.

That purpose is your power.
Let it lead the way.
Reprogramming is a must.
Changing yourself.
Integrating your pain.
Until you are whole.
When you are whole,
Your purpose will come.
The meaning of life,
It is there for you.
Your soul will find meaning.
Once you start to believe.
Believe in yourself,
All the way.
Finding your worth.
Taking a risk,
And losing it all.
Leaving your comfort.
Leaving a world,
That was never yours.
Open your eyes.
You are seeing it all.
That illusion is gone.
Your mask,
You can take off.
Being what everyone else wants you to be.
That is in the past.
You are free.
You are you.
You are safe now.
You have stopped pleasing the world.
You have stopped pretending to be,

Everything you're not.
Your truth comes out.
You have found your voice.
You will speak your truth.
You have found safety,
In your own body.
You have connected with your body,
And your mind.
That connection to your soul.
That is what you have done.
Change needed to come.
Disruption and havoc.
Chaos and pain.
Emotions and darkness.
This bridge of in between.
In between your old world.
This darkness and confusion.
Before you find bliss.
No one understands.
You are on your own.
It is lonely here.
You have learned to just be.
Just be here.
Nothing to fix.
Drop your control.
You have found surrender.
You have picked up faith,
To carry you through.
You are sitting in the dark.
All by yourself.
Going through all of the layers.
Letting yourself feel.

Feeling these emotions.
The darkness will pass.
It always does.
You have come to know so many storms.
You have come to be okay,
With disappointment and let downs.
This is what comes,
When you learn to let go.
You have learned to stand next to fear.
This fear is not real.
It comes to keep you,
In your old world.
Bring this with you.
This fear is here.
You can walk with it,
Without pushing it away.
This is all part of your healing journey.
Love and acceptance.
This appears too.
Letting the darkness flow,
As you find the light.
There must be darkness,
In order to uncover the light.
There must be stillness,
To appreciate movement.
This light is your soul.
Your soul is waiting.
Waiting for you.
Waiting for you to walk this journey.
This journey for you.
This journey is yours.
This path of waves.

Let these waves come.
Waves of emotion.
You are no longer stoic.
Drop this guard.
Let down your walls.
This protection you've had.
It is no longer yours.
You don't need it,
Not anymore.
You have found trust in yourself.
These storms have given you,
Tools you need.
Tools you will need to find love for yourself.
These storms have come,
To show you love.
Love for yourself.
Your one true love.
It is you.
Unconditional love.
This is the journey.
You've uncovered your gifts along the way.
Your gift of empathy.
Your gift of compassion.
Your gift of understanding.
Your gift of becoming conscious.
These gifts you will hold.
You will hold them close.
This is your gift,
You give to the world.
This is your contribution.
This deep, dark journey.
It will all be worth it.

When you are standing at the end,
Looking back.
Looking at all you've accomplished,
And never losing hope.
This hope you hold.
Never let it go.
This hope will lead you to where you need to go.
This hope.
This faith.
This what you will give.
Give to others,
Who are also on this path.
We are all connected.
We are all one.
This path of healing.
This lifestyle of healing.
Spread this out.
Spread it along.
Keep connecting.
You are healing the world.

My Soul

My soul.
I hear you.
These layers,
I have removed.
These layers were keeping me from you.
My soul.
I see you.
I see you so clear.
With this,
I found clarity.
The blur is gone.
My soul.
I feel you.
I feel the enlightenment.
I feel the bliss.
I feel the love.
I feel the gratitude.
I feel goosebumps,
On my skin.
I feel my spirituality.
My soul.
I understand you.
I finally understand.
I understand the darkness.
I understand the pain.
I understand the layers that were in the way.
I understand the grief.
My soul.
I have carried you, all of this time.
I didn't know it.

I couldn't hear it.
I couldn't see it.
I couldn't feel it.
I couldn't understand it.
My soul.
You've been here all along.
You were protected by my walls.
Protected by a shield.
I was not connected.
Connected to you.
I was living a life,
That was not in alignment with you.
As I uncovered the layers.
I started to understand,
This place I was in.
Was not for you.
Your calling,
I heard.
Your calling,
I felt.
I sacrificed a lot,
To discover my soul.
I sacrificed a whole life,
That I had built.
I've walked away,
To find what is meant for me.
I'm connected now,
To my soul.
My soul will lead the way.
My soul will guide my path.
My soul will find direction.
My soul will discover my purpose.

This discovery will come,
I know it and trust it.
I have complete trust in you,
My beloved soul.

This Inner Girl

This inner girl.
She is speaking loud.
Loud enough to hear.
Loud enough to feel.
I see her now.
This clarity of her.
This inner girl,
She found her voice.
She found her feelings.
She found her truth.
She found what was hiding.
She found the illusions.
She found the root.
The root of her pain.
She now has a voice.
She speaks so clear.
She will make it known,
Each time she feels.
She will make it known,
Each time she wants to speak.
My job,
Is to honor her.
Let her come out.
I have freed her,
From the cage she was in.
She now feels safe.
Safe,
In my arms.
This inner girl,
She found her home.

I am her home.
I am her safety.
I am her freedom.
I love her.
All this time,
She's been looking for love.
Love that was not mine.
Love that was on the outside.
This love she needed.
It was always mine.
My love to give her.
This is what she needed.
She needed me.
This whole time.
I needed to learn her.
I needed to hear her.
I needed to see her.
I needed to love her.
She just needed love.
Love from me.
It was always this easy,
But so hard to find.
We had to go through layers.
Layers of pain.
All of these layers,
Were keeping her from love.
These layers,
Peeling back.
Brought her closer to love.
This love from me.
This inner girl,
We are so close.

We are so connected.
Together we love.
We love each other.
This inner girl,
She used to be a whisper.
Her voice was a whisper,
Because she didn't believe.
She didn't believe that she had any worth.
The more I listened.
The more I paid attention.
Her worth became more.
She started to believe.
Believe in herself.
Her voice became louder.
She had faith in her actions.
This inner girl,
Has found her worth.
This worth will never be taken away.
This worth in her,
It is here to stay.
Never again,
Will the outside world have an effect.
Have an effect,
On her again.
She stands grounded.
This inner girl,
She found love in me,
And love in herself.

The Greatest Gift Of All

They don't like hearing it.
Hearing the truth.
They don't like her words.
Her words that she speaks.
She speaks the truth.
She says what is true.
They say she's too blunt.
They say she's too much.
She says it like it is.
She will call you out.
She is not afraid.
Afraid of the games.
She just won't play them.
Games are fake.
She doesn't do fake.
Not anymore.
She won't take part.
She won't let it slide.
She let too much slide.
Once before.
She will catch it as it comes.
She will hold them accountable.
She will not sacrifice herself.
She will choose herself,
Every single time.
What she says,
Makes them uncomfortable.
What she does,
Bothers them more.
They are so concerned,

With everyone but themselves.
They can't hold space,
For what she has to say.
They can't go there,
And that's okay.
It's not her concern,
Not anymore.
She used to be bothered.
She used to care.
Cared what they thought.
Thought of her.
Until she realized,
The only thing that matters.
Is her opinion of herself.
They can judge.
They can talk.
Talk about her.
She will shrug it off.
What they say.
It has more to do with them,
Anyways.
They say she's harsh.
They say she's too picky.
She goes on dates,
And nothing works.
Let them judge.
Let them talk.
She just won't settle.
She can be alone.
Alone with herself.
Herself,
She loves.

This love that she has,
For herself.
This love,
Wasn't always there.
This love for herself,
Came after so much hurt.
So much hurt,
That she endured.
Her love was given.
Given away freely.
She opened her heart.
Her whole heart was open.
She gave her love.
All of it away.
But she didn't leave any for herself.
She started to notice.
She needed love.
She deserved the love she was giving away.
She gave it away,
Without knowing.
Knowing how much she needed it.
She started to give.
Give love to herself.
She realized she had never done this before.
She started to treat herself.
Like she did everyone else.
Nurture and love.
Kindness and care.
She finally felt like she mattered.
She mattered and was important.
She deserved to receive.
She can receive,

And not just give.
She can receive,
Receive from herself.
Receive this love,
That she so freely gave away.
This love for herself,
She had never seen.
She had never known,
This feeling before.
This emotional work.
This work that she has done.
It affected others,
That were receiving her love.
As she came out with her truth,
Many would leave.
They didn't know what to do.
They didn't know how to handle this girl.
This girl with self-love.
This girl who got to know herself.
This girl who stopped sacrificing herself.
Her relationships fell apart.
They wanted that old girl back.
The girl who gave,
Everything she had.
The girl who broke her back,
To please everyone else.
The girl who pleased,
Everyone but herself.
She gave and gave,
Until there was nothing left.
Those around her,
Left feeling good.

She gave this love,
For them to be filled up.
They all were filled up,
And she was empty.
She thought this was her job.
She didn't know.
She didn't know,
That love for herself.
Was just as important as giving it out.
This felt selfish.
Selfish at first.
Until she realized.
How can she love anyone else,
If she can't even have love for herself?
It was selfish of her.
Selfish to her own self.
Selfish to give,
All of her love away.
This was an act of self-betrayal.
This was an act of self-abandonment.
This was an act of self-sacrifice.
This was an act of self-sabotage.
This was an act,
She would have to undo.
Undo this over giving.
Balance it out.
She needed to find balance.
Balance for herself.
She needed to find,
Her true self.
She needed to find,
The greatest gift.

The greatest gift of all.
The greatest gift she will ever receive.
This gift of love,
Given by her and received by her.

My Calls

Hi.
I am seen.
I am heard and understood.
I feel good.
I feel loved now that you see who I am.
I can't believe it has been all this time.
I have been trying to get ahold of you for years.
I have been calling and calling.
Knocking and shouting.
You have been ignoring my calls,
All this time.
What made you pick up this time?
What made you answer?
Was it that you were alone with me,
Long enough?
You finally made time for me.
You finally made room.
I am thankful for this,
You have no idea.
You have no idea,
How much it means.
Means to me that I feel seen.
I feel important now.
I feel like a person now.
I finally feel loved.
Loved by you.
My calls have been answered.
Answered by you.
You are finally listening.
I finally feel heard.

I finally feel understood.
What took so long?
What took you so long?
I have been calling.
Calling for years.
I have been reaching out.
I have been calling you.
Calling you to help.
Calling you to listen.
To listen to all of the times,
I felt hurt.
I needed you to listen to all of the times,
I felt unsafe.
I was ignored because of the chaos.
The noise of the chaos kept me from you.
The distractions.
The noise.
Your old life.
Busy.
Busy.
Busy.
Always stay busy.
Keep going.
Don't stop.
Care for everyone else.
I am so thankful for the day.
The day you stopped.
The day you stopped running.
Running from me.
Running from my calls.
You finally heard me.
You heard my call.

It was actually a shout.
Your back gave out.
Your health was affected.
This was my shout.
My shout to you.
I wanted you to hear me.
I wanted you to see me.
I just needed to feel my feelings.
My feelings,
I shoved down.
I shoved them away,
Because I didn't feel safe.
I shoved them away,
To build a life.
A life that wasn't ours.
A life that we needed to leave.
We needed a new start.
You finally listened.
I am so thankful that you are hearing me now.
I am so thankful that you are seeing me now.
I am so thankful that you answered my call.
My calls went unanswered,
For so long.
I have been inside you all this time.
Waiting to be seen.
Waiting to be heard.
Waiting to be understood.
We needed alone time.
We needed each other.
We needed to reconnect with each other.
We needed this discovery.
This discovery time.

This time spent alone.
Quiet and peaceful.
Solitude and rest.
Thank you finally,
For answering my call.
Thank you,
I love you.

Empath

She is an empath.
She can feel your emotions.
She can feel your energy.
She can feel when you are processing.
She can sense when you need to be alone.
She can sense your needs.
She can sense your mood.
She can feel a shift.
A shift in your mood.
A shift in the air.
A shift in the environment.
A shift in nature.
She is sensitive.
She is genuine.
She listens to her intuition.
She can read the room.
She can read you.
She knows if you are sad.
She knows if you are angry.
She knows if you are in pain.
She knows when you are lying,
And when you speak the truth.
She can truly understand.
Understand what you are going through.
She can guess when you are off.
She knows when something isn't right.
She can predict scenarios before they happen,
She can feel it in her gut.
She has obscene amounts of empathy.
She can feel what you feel in her body.

Bring her to someplace quiet.
Quiet and nature.
No loud noises.
No more noise.
Just the sounds of nature and birds.
The sounds of waves breaking on the beach.
Connecting with nature,
Brings her to her soul.
She connects with herself,
Under the soft glow of the sun.
Nature is healing.
Nature is recharging.
She is an empath.
She holds a gift.
Her gift of empathy,
That she gives to the world.
She needs to take care of herself,
Doing what she loves.
Her gift of connection,
That people love.
Her healing energy,
That brings people up.
Her healing energy,
That she spreads to the world.
Her gift of intuition,
That she will give out.
She is an empath.
Her gift of empathy,
Is something she will give.
She needs nothing in return,
Just to know you feel understood.
She wants you to feel seen.

She wants you to feel heard.
She will hold space for you.
She will hold space for your pain.
She is completely genuine,
She has no room for fake.
She won't do small talk.
She will not play games.
She can't pretend.
She is an empath.
Her gift is love.
She is not here to judge.
She just wants you to be you.
Please let her be her.
She is an empath,
She is here for the love.

Listening To My Soul

I can feel my future.
My future is close.
I can feel it in my soul.
I am listening.
Listening to my soul.
I am in tune with myself,
Like never before.
I have a knowing.
A knowing in me.
This deep knowing,
That keeps following me.
I know something is coming for me.
I know that there is something waiting for me.
I can feel this.
I feel it in my soul.
I can feel it so clear,
I feel it in my bones.
My soul.
My destiny.
Whatever is for me.
This is what I feel.
Deep within me.

Judgement

They don't know what to do with you now.
They don't know how to handle you now.
They don't know how to communicate with you.
They don't know what happened to you.
It's so easy to judge.
Judge someone.
Judge them without going through,
What they've been through.
It's so easy for them,
To talk about you.
It's so easy for them,
To judge you.
Judge your actions.
Judge your words.
Judge your life.
It is so easy for them,
To hate on you.
Hate on you,
Without being you.
It is so easy for them,
To sit there and judge.
Judge the way,
You choose to live.
Judge the way,
You choose to walk away.
It is not them,
Who lived your pain.
It is not them,
Who saw what you saw.
It is not them,

Who was beaten down.
It is not them,
Who was betrayed.
It is not them,
Who walked away.
Walked away from all that you knew.
It is not them,
Who did this.
It was you.
So let them talk.
Let them be.
Let them judge.
Let them hate.
They are not the ones,
Who were forced to change.
They were not the ones,
Who lived your life.
They just don't know what happened to you.
They just don't have an easy answer.
An answer that makes sense.
Makes any sense to them.
This is something that really can't be explained.
Explained to them.
This process.
This pain.
This path you are on.
This is not something that you planned.
This is not something that you asked for.
This is not something that can be explained.
This is just something,
That just is.
It is what it is,

And it cannot be changed.
The path you are on,
It is very easy to judge.
It is easy to sit there,
On the outside.
It is easy to judge,
When it's not your ride.
It is easy to judge,
When you don't carry pain.
It is easy to judge,
When you are not aware.
It is easy to judge,
When you don't have to grieve.
After moving through all of this,
You will never judge anyone again.
You see people different now.
You see people's pain.
You understand why they are the way they are.
You will find empathy.
You will understand.
You will never carry judgement in your heart.

This Water

This water.
It flows.
It flows around me.
This water.
It's soft.
It is gentle.
It flows.
This water,
It changes.
It is constantly changing.
Changing with the breeze.
Changing with the wind.
This water,
These waves.
These waves that break.
Breaking on the shore,
At my feet.
This water,
I feel.
This water is peace.
This water flows.
Flows around me.
This water is healing.
This water brings bliss.
This water is calm.
This water washes up at my feet.
This water removes toxicity.
This water heals.
This water mends.
This water removes negative energy.

Wash away now.
Wash it all away now.
Refresh.
Clear.
This water revives.
Revives me.

This Moment Is Mine

This moment,
Right now.
It is so perfect.
This moment,
The sun.
The sun on my face.
This moment,
The grass.
The grass touches my feet.
This moment,
Right now.
The birds,
They chirp.
The sounds of the birds.
The flowers,
By my side.
The smell of the flowers.
The wind.
The breeze.
The soft summer air.
Breathe in.
Breathe out.
This moment I am In.
This moment I feel.
This moment is mine.
This moment is all I really have.
This moment,
Right now.
The simple life.
It's truly amazing.

It's simple.
It's nothing.
It's peaceful.
It's quiet.
This moment,
Right now.

Drop It All

Drop the weight.
Put it all down.
None of it is yours.
Empty it out.
Forget the stories.
Drop the words.
The words that were spoken.
Spoken to you.
Forget society.
Forgive the abuse.
Lose those expectations.
Expectations of you.
Feel your emotions.
Rest your body.
Let it all go.
Keep emptying it out.
This weight is not yours.
You deserve to be free.
Shine your light.
Take care of yourself.
Speak your truth.
Become authentic.
Keep it moving,
And don't look back.
Feel the grief.
This grief will come.
From everything you let go,
And everything you've dropped.
The beliefs you have.
They are not real.

They are limiting and old.
They are from your past.
You don't need them anymore.
Create new beliefs.
Beliefs that are yours.
Not what society says,
And not what will be approved.
Approval belongs to you,
Not to anyone else.
Let them judge.
Let them talk.
Let them criticize,
And then brush it off.
The words they say,
Have more to do with them anyways.
Your road is yours,
And it is up to you to pave it.
Get rid of your attachments,
Detach from it all.
The only validation you need,
Is your own.
You've stopped looking for it externally.
You found your confidence.
You filled your void.
You dealt with your suppressed emotions.
You stay true to yourself now.
You have stopped putting yourself aside.
You have learned self-care.
You have opened your heart.
You have connected to your body.
You found your self-awareness.
You have embraced your flaws.

You found your trauma,
And you sat with it all.
You heard your little girl,
You will never neglect her again.
You chose trust over control.
You left all of the plans.
You removed the distractions.
You let yourself feel.
You changed your world.
You stopped putting your worth,
In other people's hands.
You trust yourself now,
More than ever before.
You connect with nature.
You dropped all of the weight.
You removed the barricades,
That were standing in your way.
You stopped being the doormat,
For everyone's problems.
You started speaking up,
Instead of sitting with it.
Wasting your time,
Trying to figure it out yourself.
Using up your energy,
And leaving nothing left for you.
You found peace,
After all the chaos.
It was in that chaos,
That you figured it out.
Figured out that you did not belong.
The only place you belong,
Is your own self-love.

I Will Hold My Heart

To all of our people that are no longer here,
With us by our sides.
To all of our people we remember,
That had to leave us too soon.
To all of our people that took their own lives.
To all of you,
That are no longer here.
To all of your souls and spirits,
That still linger near.
I want you to know,
I see you still.
I hear your voice.
And I feel your presence.
You are still here,
With me
Always.
You are here in my heart.
You are here in my mind.
You are here in my spirit.
You are here in my soul.
You will never be forgotten.
You will never be gone.
Your face I still see.
Your voice I still hear.
Your soul resides within me.
I reach for you,
You are so far away.
I reach for you,
Because I know you are not gone.
You are just a soft wind.

A wind that blows in the air.
A wind that comes,
With every storm.
A wind that is here,
On a soft summer day.
A wind that is near,
It'll never fade.
You are here.
I feel you still.
And that will always be.
The love that you gave,
It is here, it is inside of me.
And that'll never change.
The love that you were,
Will never be gone.
Because love is something that will linger on.
I want you to know,
Your spirit is still here.
It is inside of my heart.
And anytime I miss you,
I put my hand up on my chest.
And I hold you near.
I hold you so close,
I can almost feel your breath.
Because that is love.
And love is so strong,
It lives in our hearts.
And that is what I hold.
I hold it anytime,
I need to remember.
I hold it when I need you,
I hold it when I am sad.

I hold it when I can't go on,
I hold it just to feel you.
I hold it when I feel like I've forgotten.
I remember our memories.
I remember our days.
I remember all our laughs.
And each time I hold my heart,
Inside of my hands...
It is you that is here once again.
It all comes back.
Every single time,
I hold my heart in my hands.
I can bring you back,
Anytime I need.
And that is what I know,
And trust completely.
I know that love is strong,
And will live on...
Until the end of time.
And even though you are not here now,
Your love will never leave.
I will hold my heart,
Inside of my hands and bring you back.
And even though you left too soon,
You left this love behind.
I will hold it,
In my heart.
And never let it go.

In My Element

In my element.
Sitting in serenity.
Peace,
By the water.
Calm and quiet.
Nothing but wind.
Wind and waves.
The birds are here.
This is my element.
This is where I belong.
I belong right here.
No distractions.
Nothing to do.
Stillness and solitude.
The noise is gone.
Distractions and chaos,
Are so far away.
I am in my element.
Right where I belong.
The clouds,
Up above me.
The beautiful sky.
The colors of the sunset.
The warm summer breeze.
The flowers are blooming.
The grass is growing.
The vines on the fence.
Everything is so green.
Notice my surroundings.
Notice nature.

The roses.
The lilies.
The hydrangeas and lavender.
The ferns.
The plants.
I notice it all.
This is peace.
This is my element.

Walking Away...

When you walk away,
You make space.
You make space,
For what is right.
What is right for you.
You will fill this space,
With your own self-love.
You make space for more connection.
Connection that suits who you are now.
Walking away.
Saying goodbye.
Letting go.
These are all signs,
That you are making space.
Empty out.
As you proceed.
Proceed to let go.
Peel away each layer.
Keep peeling and peeling.
Peel back each layer.
Each layer of pain.
Let it flow throughout you.
And then release.
Release it all.
There you will be.
Your light is there.
It has been inside of you,
This whole time.
You just couldn't see.
See beyond the pain.

You just couldn't see.
Because you needed to heal.
You didn't believe.
Believe in yourself.
Covered by these layers.
That you are uncovering.
You made yourself small.
Because of the weight.
This weight you have been carrying,
All this time.
This weight kept you from your own light.
This weight kept you from your own self-love.
This weight kept you from your true self.
This weight kept you hiding.
Afraid to come out.
Come out to be who you really are.
Afraid of vulnerability.
Afraid to be judged.
Afraid to be rejected.
Afraid that you won't be accepted.
It is when you stop hiding.
It is when you take your power back.
It is when you speak your truth,
That you find where you belong.
Follow your heart.
Trust in yourself.
Walking away is hard,
But you can't carry this weight.
Set it all down.
Listen to your gut.
Listen for your spirit.
Leaving what you know,

Detaching from the outcome.
Letting go of any attachment,
Makes room for unconditional love.

My Own Voice

Whenever I speak my truth.
Speak what is real.
What is direct.
My fear comes in.
My limiting believes,
They are all here.
This voice wants to keep me safe.
"I am here to protect.
Stay small.
Don't take this risk."
Using my voice to speak my needs.
Speak my boundaries.
Speak my truth.
Take my power back.
Stand up for myself,
Putting myself out there.
This is the risk.
The risk that I take,
To become my true self.
Uncomfortable.
Going against the norm.
I don't need to fit in.
I don't need to be liked.
But this voice will creep in.
This voice of fear.
This voice wants to keep me here.
Keep me right here.
Right here in one spot.
Pulling me back.
Keeping me comfortable,

In my comfort zone.
"Don't move from here.
Stay right here.
Don't follow your dreams.
Just keep on doing whatever you are doing.
Because it is safe."
This is what I hear.
I won't grow here.
Each time I speak my truth.
Each time I move into discomfort.
Each time I take a risk.
Each time I don't follow the rules.
But whose rules are these?
Society's?
Opinions?
Judgements?
Put downs?
There are no rules.
There are no expectations.
There is no right or wrong.
My heart will lead.
My heart will guide me.
I listen closely.
My own voice will take over.
My own voice will be louder.
My own voice is in charge.
My own voice I will hear.
I choose my own voice,
Over this voice of fear.

Do Not Say A Word

It was morning.
A sunny morning.
Leaving for the gym.
Backing up in the driveway.
There was a man.
A man with his car.
He blocked me in.
A man with a gun.
A gun to my head.
This man with the gun.
He said to me,
To make a call.
I stayed calm.
I didn't even flinch.
I spoke to him,
In my normal voice.
I made the call,
And he held the gun.
I made the call,
I said a few words.
I hung up the phone.
He took the gun down.
This man with the gun.
He walked away.
He got in his car.
He drove away.
He drove his car away.
This man with the gun.
I was left in my car,
In disarray.

I didn't know what had just happened.
I went into shock.
I put the car in reverse,
And off I went.
I went off,
That day.
And proceeded,
As normal.
I did not speak of this event,
At all that day.
I did not speak of this event,
For many years.
I did not speak of this event,
Because I blocked it all out.
Pushing it so far down,
That it will never come up.
Shove it and push it.
Block it completely out.
I blocked it out because I did not know what to do.
I blocked it out because I was afraid.
I blocked it out because...
Oh my god.
Did that really happen?
I just went into shock.
I was scared.
Scared of this man.
I was scared of him,
Coming back.
I was told not to say a word.
Do not say a word,
I was told this so many times.
This is what I did,

To survive.
Do not say a word...
Not to anyone.
Do not go for help...
Do not stand up for yourself.
Do not say a word,
Hold your feelings in.
Hold in all of your feelings,
And do not say a word.
Do not open your mouth.
Do not ever get help.
Do not stand up for yourself.
I did not say a word,
Because who would I tell?
Every time I went for help,
I was shut down.
So, keep my mouth shut,
And live my life.
Just keep going,
Stay in survival mode.
And do not say a word.
Once I say a word,
This event becomes real.
If I speak these words,
I would have to deal.
Deal with the emotions.
The emotions I shoved away.
I could not say a word,
Because I did not feel safe.
Do not ever say a word.
That is how I lived,
For so many years.

This is how lived,
Holding everything in.
This is not how I will live,
Not anymore.
The way I used to live,
Is just not okay.
Surrounded with people,
Who did not keep me safe.
Surrounded with people,
Who did not listen to me.
Surrounded with people,
Who dismissed me.
Surrounded with people,
Who told me to not say a word.
Surrounded with people,
Living in a façade.
Surrounded with people,
Who only thought about themselves.
Surrounded with people,
Who manipulated me.
I just did what I was told,
Out of fear.
I did what I was told,
Because I was used to being controlled.
I just did what I was told,
To not rock the boat.
I did what I was told,
To please everyone else.
Pleasing everyone else,
Was my role.
This is not my role,
Not anymore.

I will do what I want now,
Not what I am told.
I will love myself now,
I will listen to myself now.
I do what I want now.
I will open my mouth now,
I will speak my truth now.

Curled up

Put this weight away.
Empty yourself out.
Carry this away.
Cleanse yourself.
Put this weight down.
This weight you've been carrying.
Feel this pain.
Let it all come.
Let it all leave.
This weight.
This pain.
Put it all down.
You are cleansed.
You are lighter,
Than ever before.
You deserve this.
Feel this pain.
Curl up into a ball.
Don't try to run.
Sit back down.
Curl back up.
Feel this pain.
The only way out is through.
No one can help you through this...
No one, but you.
You are the answer.
You are the one.
Stop finding distractions.
Stop finding something to do.
Stop avoiding the problem.

The problem is inside of you.
Curl up into that ball.
Curl up and feel.
Curl up and hold yourself.
Curl up and let it go.
The only way out,
Is through.
Through this pain.
Feel this.
Empty out.
Put this weight away.
Curl back up.
Back into this ball.
This ball that you were in.
This little ball makes you feel safe.
Stay there now.
All curled up.
Stay here with yourself...
With your pain.
Let those tears come,
As you stay in this ball.
Stay curled up.
This is just what you need.
All curled up,
Into this ball.

Direct Words

My direct words are not meant to hurt you.
My direct words are for clarity.
Clear and direct.
So, there is no confusion.
Up front and honest.
My words are genuine.
Direct and clear.
To the point.
This is how it is.
My words,
Are not meant to hurt you.
My words are truthful.
Sometimes the truth hurts.
Reality without the illusion.
My words are truthful.
Honest and genuine.
They are not coated with sugar,
Or perfection.
They are not coated with that illusion.
These real words help to remove the illusion.
The illusion you have there for protection.
Protection from the truth.
Protection from reality.
Your armor.
Words that are coated.
Direct communication are words without the illusion.
Words that are clear.
There is no confusion.
Direct communication paired up with presentation.
Direct words paired with empathy and compassion.

It is how you present,
These direct words.
Presentation is important.
Direct.
Clear.
Genuine,
To the point.
I prefer this,
Over the guessing.
This guessing game.
What does that mean?
The confusion.
Words that don't make any sense.
Phrases that I need to guess.
Guess what you are trying to say.
What do you mean?
Let's just be clear and direct.

The 4 Basic Needs

The 4 basic needs of a human being.
To feel appreciated.
To feel heard.
Understood and seen.
To see someone.
To really see them.
It is to see them,
Without them having to explain.
To hear them.
It is to hear them when they speak.
Hear their words and just hold space.
Listen closely.
Listen to them.
Listen to their words,
Without taking what they say personally.
Their words that they say,
Have to do with them...
Not you.
To understand them,
It is to use your empathy to meet them there.
Meet them where they are at.
Understand,
What if this was you?
Understand when they need space.
Understand when they use their voice.
How can I hear them?
Let them feel heard.
Understand when they need to grow.
Space and distance are needed to grow.
Understand their road.

Understand their ways.
Understand their process.
Appreciate them.
Really appreciate them.
Appreciate their person.
Appreciate what they bring.
Appreciate the love that they give.
Appreciate them for who they are.
Including their flaws.
Including their gifts.
The gifts they have.
The gifts they spread.
Spread to the world.
Appreciate their light.
These basic needs,
Are not hard to give.
To see with your eyes.
To hear with your ears.
Understand with your soul.
Appreciate with your heart.
Be a safe space,
With these 4 basic needs.
To show up and give these 4 basic needs.
To see.
To hear.
To understand.
To appreciate.
All of these,
Give them away.
Give them away to the people in your life.
Give them away in your relationships.

The Script

If I didn't follow the script.
The script they gave me.
If I didn't obey.
Obey their rules.
If I didn't stay.
Stay in the cage.
Stay in the cage and follow the script.
If I didn't use the words,
They needed to hear.
If I didn't obey each and every rule.
If I didn't stay...
Stay where they told me to stay.
Like a dog.
On a leash.
They had the leash.
The leash of control.
I am on a leash.
A leash held by them.
If I didn't do,
What they expected me to do.
A punishment was coming or I would be scolded.
If I didn't follow the script.
The script they gave.
If I didn't agree to be an extension of them.
If I didn't give them everything they want.
If I didn't fill their void.
If I removed myself,
To take care of me.
God forbid I give anything to myself.
I was there to give them love.

I was there to fill their cup.
I was there to meet their needs.
I was there to give,
But only to them.
They had ownership.
Ownership of me.
They weren't there to cheer me on.
They weren't there to let me be.
They certainly weren't there to meet my needs.
If they did do for me,
They expected something in return.
They are there,
But only if I follow their script.
They are there,
For their own gain.
They do for me,
But then I must do for them.
They can't give just to give.
Love on conditions.
Conditions they set.
Love on conditions,
With resentment.
They'll throw back in my face,
Everything they have ever done.
Because they did not give out of love.
They gave,
Expecting something in return.
"Look at all we've done for you."
This was thrown out at me,
While I was sitting in that cage.
It was all about them,
And what they need.

Not open to change.
Not open to learn.
Learn the new me,
That would soon emerge.
This black and white world.
I had to get out.
Get out of that cage.
Break free from that leash.
Like a dog,
Kept and controlled.
No freedom given.
Given to me.
Never understood.
If I don't follow their script...
I don't have my own mind.
I must always remember,
They are in control.
Control of the script.
Control of me...
I must not change.
I must always stay the same.
And stay in that cage.
That cage for me.
They gave me this cage,
Oh... how lucky I am.
This time.
Their script.
I receive it and leave.
Rip it to shreds,
I throw it away.
I look over my shoulder,
At that control.

I see that cage.
That leash.
That script.
I leave it all behind,
As I walk away.
Walk away from it all.
I vow to myself,
Never again will I follow a script.

Crashing Down

I watched everyone else build up their life.
Build their life to be what they wanted.
I watched and supported everyone else,
All while mine came crashing down.
Crashing down,
My whole world.
My whole world shattered,
It's gone.
How did this happen?
Where do I begin?
Where do I start?
What do I do?
How do I do this?
I built my own world,
All for it to come crashing down.
I built and built.
I loved and loved.
It didn't matter,
It still came crashing down.
Crashing down.
My whole world is gone.
I couldn't see then,
That this was part of my path.
I was going down the wrong path.
This path was not mine.
My world came crashing down,
To stop me from proceeding.
Proceeding down a path,
That was not meant for me.
I can see this now.

I understand this now.
I was in a world,
That I didn't belong in.
A world of façades.
A world of masks.
A world of external validation.
A world of control.
A world of pleasing and sacrificing yourself.
This world of black and white.
It is either this way or that way.
No in between.
This world I was in.
Leaving this world,
Meant leaving behind.
Leaving behind,
Parts of me.
Parts of me,
That I had never seen.
Parts of me,
That I had dismissed.
Parts of me,
That I never knew existed.
I started looking in the mirror.
I started looking within.
These parts of me,
Needed attention.
These parts of me,
Needed love.
Love and nurture.
Rest and revival.
Solitude and recharge.
My new world is peaceful.

My new world full of color.
It started with greys,
And now every single color.
It started from darkness,
And now I am sitting with light.
The death of illusions.
The death of denial.
The death of my mask.
The death of my façade.
So much grieving,
Feeling every emotion.
Every emotion,
I ever put away.
Put away,
To not feel.
Put away,
To not see.
Pretend it is not there.
Put it aside,
And just keep going.
Limiting beliefs,
Holding me back.
Creating new beliefs,
That would open my heart.
Connecting with my body,
To keep my heart open.
Keeping my heart open,
Led to my soul.
Here I am,
Connected to my soul.
Speaking these words now.
These words...

"I am thankful for the darkness."
"I am thankful for my world falling apart."
"I am thankful for my old world,
Because without it, I would not be here."

This Expansion

This wounded place.
This wound in me.
This black gaping hole was filled with betrayal.
Carrying this around.
Around in me,
Carrying this darkness.
Carrying this weight.
Carrying this pain.
This pain I felt.
I felt this rip.
This rip in my heart.
I heard this rip.
I heard it tear.
I felt this expansion.
This expansion in my chest.
This expansion of betrayal.
This part of my heart,
I had never felt.
I closed my eyes because I could not see.
I could not feel into this.
I could never have understood.
Understood this pain I felt.
This pain I shoved.
I shoved it away.
I shoved it away until I had the tools.
Until I had the space.
The space to give.
The space to hear.
Hear this pain.
This pain in me.

I needed to listen to this inner voice.
I needed to listen to my own voice.
"You need to cry.
You just need to cry."
Nothing else.
Please feel into this.
Feel into this pain.
Feel into yourself.
You had never seen.
Seen this pain.
Trying to be seen,
By everyone else.
But all you needed,
This whole time.
All you needed was yourself.
You just needed you.
You needed to be held.
Nothing to do.
Nowhere to go.
Just sit in this expansion.
This expansion of betrayal.
You were betrayed,
So many times.
Loved on conditions.
Loved with transactions.
This broken heart.
This rip I felt.
I felt it tear,
So, I could mend and repair.
I cried these tears,
So, the pain would leave.
I cried these tears,

To acknowledge me.
Acknowledge this part of me,
I had never seen.
"Once she felt seen,
Her love arrived.
This love for herself.
It filled this space.
This big black hole,
Is now filled with love.
This place that only knew dark.
The dark was removed and replaced with light.
This light of love.
This love for herself."

This Black Hole

You just needed to be seen.
You needed to be heard.
You needed to be understood and loved.
You just needed nurturing.
You just needed you.
You just need to cry.
Cry and forgive.
Forgiveness will lead.
Lead to love.
Forgiveness will lead.
Lead to the light.
The light is you.
This light of love.
You were buried.
Buried underneath your pain.
This crack.
This shadow,
You have never seen.
You had never seen her.
You had no idea.
You had no idea she was even there.
Waiting for you.
Waiting to be held.
This crack in your heart.
This crack of betrayal.
You finally sat.
Sat in this darkness.
This darkness.
This disturbance.
This huge black hole.

This hole of betrayal.
This hole led you to the light.
This light of love.
This love is you.

Too Much

They say I'm too much.
I say too much.
I notice too much.
I go too deep.
But guess what,
That's me.
I'm not going to change myself.
I'm not going to make myself small.
I'm not going to make myself less.
Less than I am.
I did that for too many years,
I am not doing that again.
I will not become small,
Just for you to feel comfortable.
I won't apologize for being me.
I like to go deep.
And that is me.
That is who I am.
I love self-awareness.
I love deep conversations.
I enjoy learning about myself.
I won't walk on eggshells.
I won't be put down.
I won't be criticized and shamed.
I know,
Those behaviors come from your own insecurities.
I know my flaws.
I am aware of where I am insecure.
I know what my needs are.
I know when to retreat,

So that I won't project.
Project on to you.
I won't be pulled down.
Pulled down to where you are.
I won't have my flaws pointed out,
Just so you won't have to look at yours.
I know what is happening,
When you put me down.
I know what is happening,
When you point out my flaws.
I know what is happening,
When you point the finger.
I know what is happening,
When you won't take accountability.
Of course,
None of it is ever your responsibility.
You do no wrong,
It is always me.
It is always me,
I am the problem.
I know where this comes from.
Now,
I know.
It took me a long time,
To figure this out.
I removed my illusion.
I removed my mask.
My rose-colored glasses had me believing.
They had me believing that it was always me.
I may be too much.
This is true.
But that's okay if I'm too much for you.

There are people that accept me for me.
There are people who love me for me.
There are people,
Who don't ever say I'm too much.
So, if you do think I'm too much,
That's okay.
There are people that appreciate my,
Too much.

Needs

Knowing your needs,
Is a skill.
A skill you learn.
Learn along the way.
Knowing what your needs are,
And communicating them.
Communication goes a long way.
Stating your needs.
Setting boundaries.
These are all signs of self-love.
Loving yourself,
Consists of stating your needs.
Knowing if you have space.
Space to give.
Your body will speak.
Your body will tell you.
Tell you everything you need to know.
Do I need self-care?
Do I need to be alone?
Do I need recharging?
Do I need to go out?
Listen to your body.
Your body tells you.
Your needs are important.
Important to know.
Your needs matter.
Stop putting them aside.
Putting them aside,
For everyone else.
Not meeting your needs,

Leads to resentment.
Resentment will start leaking out of you.
Meet your needs.
They are important.

No Labels

This emotion is good.
This emotion is bad.
Avoid feeling bad.
Avoid and distract.
But what if you stopped?
Stopped with the labels.
And you let everything just be.
Accept everything as it is.
Acceptance of it all.
Grief is a sign of love.
Disappointment is a sign of hope.
Anger is here.
Feel it leave.
Let it all come.
Let it all be.
Let it all leave.
Feelings don't need to be labeled.
They don't need to be fixed.
They don't need to be suppressed.
They don't need to be ignored.
They just need to be seen.
Seen and acknowledged.
Your feelings are here.
They are here to just be.
Accept it as it comes.
They don't need to be avoided.
They don't need to be dismissed.
They will go somewhere else,
If you don't address them.
Somewhere else in your body,

To be manifested physically.
Address them now.
See them now.
Feel them now.
Listen to them.
Let them come.
Accept them.
They are what they are.
Whatever they want to be.
They are here.
For you to hold.
Hold them.
Love them.
Please don't judge them.
They are not here to be judged.
They are here for you.
They are a part of you.
Embrace all parts.
Embrace them now.
Embrace yourself,
As you become whole.

That Girl Is Gone

That girl you want.
That girl is gone.
I see you wanting her back.
Wondering where she went.
Those are your thoughts.
I see your discomfort as you feel confused.
Feeling confused,
Because she is not there.
That girl you want...
She is gone.
That girl was the one who everyone loved.
The girl who kept everyone entertained.
The girl who became whoever you wanted her to be.
The one who made you laugh.
The funny one.
The girl who shrugged everything off.
The girl who put her life off,
Being whoever you wanted her to be.
Being the girl who would people please.
Making sure everyone was happy.
Making sure everyone was good.
Putting herself aside,
For you every time.
That girl is gone.
That girl has finally put herself first.
Doing what she loves,
And knowing her needs.
Using her voice,
Setting boundaries.
She stopped running away,

So, she could return home.
Return home to herself.
She listens closely to herself now,
Instead of hearing the world.
She used to listen to everyone else.
The noise of the world is all she heard.
Her own voice was buried inside.
Buried deep inside,
Underneath all her pain.
Her own voice is all she hears.
It is louder than ever.
It is so clear.
Breaking away from all of the illusions.
The illusions she created so she could feel safe.
The illusion she lived with.
She trusted in this.
She trusted the illusion,
Instead of herself.
This illusion kept her from seeing what's real.
This illusion kept her from what she deserves.
This illusion kept her from her own gifts.
This illusion,
She puts down.
Puts it down finally.
And now,
She starts living authentically.

My Love, Inside.

Holding my heart.
Holding my love.
My love I found for myself.
All of this love was found,
Inside of myself.
Inside of my heart.
All I ever needed,
Was inside of me all along.
Looking externally,
For love and validation.
Putting my worth in everyone else's hands.
Until the day,
I saw this light.
This light,
Inside of myself.
No,
I'm not giving away all of my love.
No,
I'm not giving away my heart.
That is not my job.
I will begin to love myself.
I will learn to hold my own heart.
I will learn to hold my own love.
I will learn, I am responsible for me.
Stop putting the blame on everyone else.
I will not be brought down by your insecurities.
I will not be talked down to.
I will feel these emotions.
I will stop hiding myself.
I will give up attachments,

And free myself.
Free myself,
From whatever is not mine.
Free myself,
To live my life.
Live my life,
As I choose.
Free myself,
To be the girl.
Be the girl,
I always was.
I can hold my heart now.
My whole heart.
I don't need any help to hold it,
Like I once did.
I didn't even know how to hold my own heart.
I taught myself.
I taught myself this.
I taught myself to hold all of my own love.
I will not go looking for it outside of me.
My love is inside.
Inside of me.
This is how I became free.

True Colors

True colors shine.
Shine in times of trouble.
In times of struggle.
In times of chaos and turmoil.
In times of stress.
Inside of the madness.
True colors show,
When you are at an all-time low.
The lowest of times,
Is when true colors shine.
Open your eyes,
Do you see those colors?
Those true colors of them?
Giving them chance after chance.
Forgive and forgive.
Keep on forgiving.
Keep on trying.
Putting in all the effort.
Can't you see the true colors in them?
Why can't you see?
Stop seeing the good,
And only the good.
It is time to see the truth.
The truth is revealed.
They have shown you who they are,
Over and over.
And still you love.
Still, you forgive.
Still, you try.
Still, you put in the effort.

The only effort is yours,
And it is never theirs.
They don't put in the effort,
Why is it always you?
When is it time?
Time to stop.
Stop putting in all the effort.
Stop over giving yourself.
Those true colors are showing.
Do you see now?
Once again,
Those colors.
Those colors in them,
They are bleeding out...
To show you what's there.
Why can't you see?
It is so clear.
Over and over.
Your body told you,
And still, you don't want to see.
You don't want to believe.
Believe that is them.
Because you painted a picture.
You painted a picture,
An illusion.
You saw the good.
You knew what you wanted them to be.
You wanted them to be this,
So, you could feel safe.
Paint this pretty picture.
This picture of them.
This is not who they are,

But this illusion is all you see.
"Please just be this person...
Please?
For me?"
Those true colors are shining.
That illusion is gone.
That illusion you painted.
Painted in your mind.
Those beliefs that you had.
Those beliefs were engrained.
Engrained in you.
To keep on forgiving.
To keep on sacrificing.
To keep on trying.
To keep on fixing.
"Maybe if I do this.
Maybe if I change.
Maybe if I become different.
Maybe if I go back.
Maybe because they said...
They told me different words this time.
Maybe because I spoke up.
Maybe because..."
Excuses.
Excuses.
Please give them up.
Stop with the maybes.
This is who they are.
This is them.
They have shown you over and over.
Over and over again.
Accept it and move on.

Those true colors are shining.
They are flashing and flashing.
This is who they are.
Proceed with caution.
This illusion you will remove.
The pretty picture you are taking down.
You will take it down,
So, you can see clearly.
This pretty picture is over.
This pretty, painted picture.
This is who they are.
Their true colors are out.
You are seeing clearly now.
Take this picture down.
This pretty picture you painted.
This pretty, little picture...
Is now raw and real.
The naked truth.
This picture looks different now.
How is this the picture?
The same picture in your mind?
Those true colors are glowing,
And this picture was just an illusion.
Your eyes are finally open now.
Your eyes can finally see now.
Your eyes see their true colors.
Your eyes see this illusion.
These true colors are revealed now.
Time to get out now.

Grudges

Grudges will eat you.
Eat you alive.
Holding a grudge is holding onto scum.
Scum in your body,
That weighs you down.
Scum that takes you over,
Sucks you dry.
Sucks the life out of you,
Sucks the good energy from you.
Scum that spreads through your body,
And bleeds out onto others.
Release the grudge.
Release the scum.
Holding this grudge won't bring you anywhere good.
Holding this grudge is holding you back.
Holding this grudge is not lifting you up.
Holding this grudge will only bring you down.
Weighing you down.
Taking away love.
Love from yourself.
Release this grudge.
I will forgive,
Because that is all I know how to do.
Forgiving everyone for bleeding into my life.
Because I understand that people aren't perfect.
People make mistakes.
Hurt people, hurt people.
This I know.
This grudge is gone.
This grudge is released.

All I know is things will never be the same.
Things are different now.
Things have changed.
This grudge I will not keep.
Keep with me.
Keep inside of me.
Get this out.
Get this grudge out.
Free myself.
Free from this grudge.

Let Them Be

Just let them be.
Let everyone be.
Let them be who they want to be.
Let them choose.
Choose what is right.
Right for their life.
They can have boundaries.
They don't have to live,
The same way you live.
They can go where they want,
Whatever they decide.
Please just allow.
Allow them to be.
Allow them to go.
Allow them to leave.
People come,
And people go.
People are not meant to stay.
Some come as lessons.
Some come as love.
Some come,
So that you can let them go.
People change,
And that's okay.
People can decide.
Decide what is best.
What is best for them.
This is a risk.
A risk that you take.
A risk that you take when you let them in.

Maybe you let them in,
Just so you can let them go.
Let them come,
Let them go.
We are all made up of energy.
We are all vibrating at different frequencies.
We are all connected.
We are all one.
Let everyone come,
Then let them all go.
They might return,
Maybe they won't.
Let it all happen,
The way it should.
Let them all come,
Let them all go.
Just as it is,
It will be.
Everything happens,
The way it should.
Let everyone in,
Let them all go.
Over and over.
Around and around.
Let everything come,
Let everything go.

Clarity

Oh, you see.
You see so clearly.
You see those intentions.
Those intentions right away.
Oh, you know.
You feel it deep inside.
Listen to that feeling.
Listen to yourself.
Your voice,
It is so clear now.
You were right all along.
Your instinct was right.
You are asking for clarity.
Clarity will come.
This is your intention now.
Asking for clarity.
Clarity for yourself.
Everything you want...
It will come.
And you will know.
You know,
When you know.
When you know,
Believe them the very first time.
The first time you see.
Not the second or third.
Certainly not the fourth.
This is what's real.
Believe them the very first time.
You see clear now.

That blurred vision.
Blurred your clarity.
Blurred your decisions.
Blurred your reality.
Not anymore.
Your lens will not be fogged.
You have cleared it off.
Cleared off the fog,
So, you could see clearly.
You get to decide now.
Listen to that first sign.
Go with your gut.
Your gut,
You know.
Extremely well.
Clarity will come,
Now that you know yourself.

Nice

The nice person.
Nice when you want something.
Nice for your own gain.
Nice while you are using me.
Using me to suit you.
Using me as an object.
Using me as a tool.
Using me to meet your needs.
Using me as a pedestal.
A pedestal to lift you up.
Using me,
To make you feel good inside.
Using me,
As your distraction.
A distraction from what is inside.
Something inside of you,
That you don't want to see.
You are operating from your ego,
This is so clear to me.
Take advantage,
Of my good side.
The good side in me doesn't see your flaws.
The good part of me finds excuses for you.
The goodness in my heart,
Isn't listening to my gut.
My gut is telling me something isn't right.
But here my heart is,
Having hope for you.
Giving you one more chance.
Another chance after that.

Chance after chance,
Until I open my eyes.
My eyes are wide open now.
Wide open to the truth.
The truth about you.
The truth comes out.
Your true colors shine.
Shining a light,
That I never saw before.
A light so bright,
That I no longer can ignore.
I sit in disbelief,
As you show me who you are.
Oh, wow.
This is you.
This has always been you.
You taking advantage.
Taking advantage of my love.
You putting me down.
Subtly...
To make you feel good.
Those very subtle put downs,
Mixed with manipulation.
Pretty words and validation,
Made me have trust in you.
Trusting in this dishonesty.
This dishonest truth that you show.
The minute I stop being at your beckon call.
The minute I stop giving you my extra love.
Extra love that I don't have to give.
That extra love,
I now give to myself.

This is the minute,
Your true colors bleed out.
They bleed out when I am knocked down.
When I am knocked down,
And you kick me down harder.
That is the minute,
I see the real you.
It is always about you.
It always was.
Everything you gave...
Was for your own gain.
You give out of expectation,
Not out of your heart.
You give so that you feel good.
You give expecting something in return.
I will learn.
Learn from this.
Learn from you.
This lesson I learn...
Is to always,
Always give from my heart.
Give out of love,
With no expectations.
Give out that pure unconditional love.
Give out of the space.
The space in my heart.
The space in my heart,
That is so completely genuine.
This genuine space to give,
Without having any expectation.
Give to just give.
Give to love.
Spread the love from my heart to yours.

All About You

That smile on your face.
The words out of your mouth.
You are so nice...
But you are so fake.
Your intentions come across,
Like you are so nice.
Your intentions come across,
Like you want to give.
Your intentions that you are painting.
Painting a picture.
Painting this picture,
That you are so nice.
Oh,
There you are.
Giving out these pretty words.
Lifting me up,
Just to get me to give.
You know I am a giver,
So, you take advantage of me.
You lie to my face,
And then cover it up.
You have me as your friend,
For your own gain.
I am your lifter.
I answer every call.
I give you so much validation.
I never let you down.
I think you are the greatest.
I give you my all.
I am there to pick you up.

Pick you up when you fall.
I check in on you.
Everything is always on your terms.
I put my life aside,
While I stand as your lifeline.
I rush to meet your needs,
I do everything I am told.
I sit on the phone for hours,
As I listen to you vent.
Trauma dumping and complaining,
Is the reason for this call.
You stop by to see me...
But it is on your terms,
Not mine.
You don't ask me questions,
To hear what I have to say.
You come from a place of needing to be needed.
You paint yourself as the victim.
I sit and listen always.
I am your person.
I hear you and see you,
I will always understand you.
I don't really have boundaries,
Not with you.
Because deep down,
I know.
I know who you are.
But I don't want to see,
I don't want to believe.
I don't want it to be true...
That the real you,
Is using me.

Using me for your own gain.
I don't realize that you are controlling me.
Controlling me,
Again...
For your gain.
So that you have power.
Power over me.
And the minute,
I stop.
The very minute,
I end this.
The very minute,
I realize.
I realize what is going on.
That is the minute,
You twist it all around.
You put it on me,
To carry this around.
This very minute,
Is when I call it all out.
That is the minute,
You deny the truth.
That is the minute,
You throw it back in my face.
This is the minute.
The minute I see.
I see you for you.
I see exactly what is happening.
Oh, it is clear.
It is SO, SO clear.
That smile on your face,
Has now turned to defense.

Those pretty words you gave,
Are now being thrown back at me.
You throw at me,
Every mistake I have ever made.
It all comes spinning back on to me.
You might say you are sorry,
Maybe you don't.
You might take accountability,
But you probably won't.
The accountability you may take,
Is probably half ass.
This accountability is fake,
Because you only used your words.
This fake accountability,
Is again to make you feel good.
It is all about you,
It always has been.
Your actions speak louder.
Your actions show me,
Everything I need to know.
I will watch for those actions.
Those actions are clear.
Clearer to me,
Than ever before.
How did I not see this?
How did I get into this?
My heart.
My big heart.
My heart got me here.
I have learned to protect it.
I will protect it better.
Protect my heart,

Is my lesson.
This lesson I have learned.
I learned from you.

I Choose Me

I choose myself.
I choose me.
Each time I choose,
I will choose myself.
This is the way,
To my own self-love.
If someone doesn't choose me,
This is a chance.
A chance to choose myself.
This is my chance,
To look at myself.
Why am I agonizing over them,
When I can choose myself?
If someone is not choosing me,
That's okay.
That's okay because,
I choose me.
I choose myself.
I will choose me.
This is the way...
The way to self-love.
This can't be found,
Externally.
Love can only be found,
On the inside.
Internally.
Inside of me.
Inside of my heart.
Look within.
Deep within.

Within myself,
Is where I find my love.
I choose me.
I choose my love.
External love,
Doesn't fulfill.
External love,
Can't cover up.
External love,
Can't replace.
External love,
Is not the quick fix.
The quick fix for my own love.
The quick fix for self-love.
External love,
Will never fill the void.
This void within me.
I must fill my void,
With my own self-love.
Self-love is found,
When I choose myself.
Once I make the choice,
I bring myself home.
Back home to my heart.
My heart,
Right where I belong.

Her Person

He was her person.
Her person she loved.
He was her person.
Her person who took up her whole heart.
He was her love.
He was her all.
Until he wasn't.
She held onto him.
Until she let go.
She held onto him for as long as she could.
She had to let him go.
She had to turn her back.
She was holding on so tight.
Too tight.
Because he was her person.
Her person she knew.
Her person.
Her safety.
Her protector.
Her love.
She had to let him go.
Because it was breaking her heart.
It was breaking her heart by holding onto him.
It was breaking her heart by holding on too tight.
She had to let go.
Let go of him.
Let go of them,
And the life that they built.
She had to make peace with him,
And what he chose.

She will never stop caring.
She will never stop loving.
But she had to let him go,
Because her heart was aching.
Aching,
Because she loved him so much.
Aching,
Because she wanted the best.
The best for him.
The best for his life.
The best for his heart.
The best for his soul.
She loved him so much,
But she had to let go.
Let go of their love.
Let go of him.
She had to choose herself.
She had to choose her own love.
She had to choose,
What was best for her.
She had to make room.
Make room for her own love.
She had to finally let go.
She had to stop holding on.
Holding onto him.
Holding onto their love.
Holding onto a life.
A life that will never be.
Holding onto this space.
This space she had for him.
They met for a reason.
He was brought to her.

She was brought to him.
"Thank you for showing me all that you did.
I hope that you know that I want what's best for you.
I hope that you know,
I pray for you every day.
It just hurt me too much,
To see you that way.
I wish you the best.
I send you my love.
I want the best for you,
That will never change.
I just had to make this choice.
This choice for me."
She whispered this,
And blew him a kiss.
She blew him a kiss,
And she finally let go.
She finally let go,
And set herself free.

This Peace I Found

This opening.
This freedom.
This forgiveness and acceptance.
This love that I have.
Have for the world.
This peace I found.
This serenity and bliss.
This came,
After so much pain.
This all came,
After so many tears.
This feeling I have now,
It glistens.
It glistens and glows,
And shines so bright.
This love I feel.
It feels so right.
This shining light.
Like I am a shining star.
This shining star,
Is love for myself.
Love my myself,
And love for the world.
This understanding and acceptance,
That I have for you.
I accept you for you,
However, you come.
I accept everything about you,
You are who you are.
I will send you love,

From afar.
From afar,
If you aren't around.
I am still connected.
Connected to you.
I will send you love,
No matter what.
I have released my grudge.
I have released my anger.
I have released resentment.
I will hold up this love.
I will hold it up,
For myself first.
Followed by love,
For you and the world.
I will fill your cup.
First comes me,
Then comes you.
If I can't fill myself up,
I won't be good for you.
Recharge myself.
Recharge my love.
I figured this out.
This came,
After ripping out my insides.
My insides on fire,
My insides that ache.
Ripping them out,
One by one.
Sorting each piece.
Each piece of pain.
Each piece of misery.

Each piece,
I pick up.
Each piece,
I look at.
I sort all of this out,
Piece by piece.
I feel it all.
Each piece is felt.
Let it all come,
Let it all leave.
This peace I found,
From the pieces I picked up.
These pieces inside,
That I kept buried.
Buried deep down,
So that I could not reach.
I could not reach,
I could not see.
I could not feel,
I was numb.
Not anymore,
This peace I found.
This light I found.
This light of love.
This love of mine.

This Place To Fall

Can I allow myself?
Myself to fall.
Fall in love.
Fall in love again?
This pain.
This grief.
I have endured.
I am ready.
Lose it all,
To fall in love.
Let down my walls.
Open my heart.
Reveal my love,
To the world.
Lose it all,
To fall in love.
My heart.
I repaired.
I felt this pain.
The agony.
I have let it all go.
I have earned a place.
A place in love.
A place to fall.
Fall in love.
This place is mine.
Mine to fall.
Fall in love.
Fall in love with myself.

My New World

I became someone else,
When I sacrificed myself.
I made everyone else happy,
By abandoning myself.
I lived for everyone around me,
While I put myself aside.
I ignored my needs,
To hand my love away.
Giving all of my love to everyone else,
And leaving nothing left for me.
I gave and gave and gave,
While I left myself empty.
Empty without love.
Love for myself.
I gave everyone my empathy,
Without giving it to myself.
I cared for everyone else,
While I left myself alone.
Alone inside,
Without any love.
Because I was giving it all away.
I didn't feel my feelings,
Because I was there for everyone else.
I would listen to their problems.
I would answer every call.
I would get up and go,
When it was asked of me.
Little did I know,
I was living for them.
I was not living for me.

I shoved my voice so far down,
That I couldn't hear it at all.
All I heard was everyone else,
And that became my way.
Listen to everyone else.
Listen to them.
My voice didn't exist.
And when it did,
It was usually shut down.
My voice was dismissed.
My voice wasn't heard.
My voice didn't matter.
So, I shoved it away.
I really believed that I must act a certain way.
A certain way,
To receive love.
You must act this way.
You must do this for me.
You must not disappoint.
You must agree with me.
And if you do speak up.
If you do act out.
If you do show yourself,
We will leave you.
We will punish and blame you.
These were my beliefs.
Beliefs engrained in me.
I was surrounded by people,
Who loved this girl.
This girl who didn't speak up.
This girl who didn't love herself.
This girl who lived for everyone else.

My world was shattered,
So that I could make my own world.
Make a world,
Where I found love.
Love for myself.
A world where I could love myself.
A world where I could use my voice.
A world where I didn't need to become someone else.
A world without punishment.
A world without abandonment.
A world without guilt trips and shaming.
A world with no expectations.
A world without control and power.
A world without lies.
My new world is beautiful.
My new world is full of understanding and compassion.
My new world is full of acceptance and love.
My new world is where I become me.

This Beauty

This beauty in me.
This beauty in you.
This beauty in this universe.
This beauty on earth.
I step on this grass,
And I feel that connection.
I feel that connection,
To the earth.
I feel that connection,
To nature.
I feel that connection,
To the sun and the moon.
I feel that connection,
With every sunrise.
I feel that connection,
With every sunset.
I feel that connection,
With all the colors of the sky.
I feel that connection,
With the stars, up above.
I feel that connection,
With the waves of the water.
I feel that connection,
With the leaves on the trees.
I feel that connection,
With that free flowing, breeze.
I feel that connection,
With the air, that I breathe.
That connection,
Is such beauty.

Nature is healing.
Nature is grounding.
Nature is beauty.
When my body,
Meets nature.
I take in this beauty.
I take in this connection.
There is nothing else like it,
It's all I can feel.
This feeling,
Is healing.
Nature is calling.
This beauty within me,
Is finally connected.

This Distance Is Beautiful

Distance yourself.
For a while.
Distance yourself from the world.
It is quiet.
You leave the noise.
Nothing to process,
Except for your inner world.
You will hear so much.
You left the chaos,
And you found peace.
You left the distractions.
Shut your phone off.
Distance yourself.
Distance yourself,
From the world.
But not from yourself.
You are closer to yourself,
Than ever before.
You hear so clear.
You are aware.
You have found peace.
The noise is gone.
Solitude is your calling.
Healing is here.
Creating a new world.
Your inner world.
Inside this cocoon.
You will blossom soon.
There is no rush.
Letting go of so much.

There is no end date.
You are just here.
Inside of your cocoon.
Releasing old wounds.
Creating new beliefs.
Everything will be new.
Just let it all go.
Release the expectations.
Get rid of any pressure.
Your new life will be,
Just letting it be.
There is no control.
Let go of the plans.
Life doesn't follow a plan,
So why should you?
Keep it simple.
You need nothing.
Nothing but your health,
And your well-being.
Your heart is more open,
Than ever before.
You are finding forgiveness.
You are finding love.
Love for yourself,
And for the world.
Unconditional love.
Love without conditions.
This distance is beautiful.

My Own Little World

This intensity of emotions.
I am different when I am in them.
I am flooded with emotion.
I can't connect with anyone.
I am so in my body.
Sometimes, this is scary.
So many emotions.
It feels overwhelming.
Sometimes, I can't sleep.
Sometimes, I have anxiety.
Sometimes, I am tired.
Sometimes, I retreat.
Retreat, into my own little world.
My own little bubble.
That I have created for myself.
It is just me and myself.
Me, myself, and I.
All of my emotions,
Are filling up inside.
I've committed to healing.
I've committed to me.
I've committed to finally,
Putting myself first.
I've committed to this bubble.
Just me and my bubble.
My own little world,
I created for myself.
This world is complete,
With all of me.
I accept all of these parts.

I accept where I am.
I don't need to always move forward.
I don't need to always take action.
I don't need to do anything.
I can just be.
Be in my bubble.
There's been so many expectations.
Expectations, put on me.
Mostly, from myself.
I can be hard on myself.
I can push too hard.
I can say "keep going."
I can keep moving,
Even when it's not good for me.
Relax a little.
It's okay.
Just be.
Calm.
Quiet.
Those expectations.
They aren't even real.
Give myself a break,
What's right for me will come.
That balance,
Of feminine and masculine energy.
Find it.
It feels good.
That balance.
Grounded.
Stay in that balance.
Remove the expectations.
Remove the pressure.

Remove it all.
Down to the bare soul.
Be in my soul.
Be there now.
I love it here.
It's quiet here.
My soul, I found it.

Make Room

When you walk away,
You make space.
You make space,
For what is right.
What is right for you.
You will fill this space,
With your own self-love.
You make room for new connections.
Connections that suit who you are now.
Walking away.
Saying goodbye.
Letting go.
These all lead to making space.
Empty out.
As you proceed.
Proceed to let go.
Peel away each layer.
Keep peeling and peeling.
Peel back each layer.
Each layer of pain.
Let it flow through you,
And then release.
Release it all.
There you will be.
Your light is there.
It has been inside of you,
This whole time.
You just couldn't see.
See beyond the pain.
You just couldn't see,

Because you needed to heal.
You didn't believe,
Believe in yourself.
Covered by these layers,
That you are uncovering.
You made yourself small,
Because of the weight.
This weight you have been carrying,
All this time.
This weight kept you from your own light.
This weight kept you from your own self-love.
This weight kept you from your true self.
This weight kept you hiding.
Afraid to come out.
Come out to be who you really are.
Afraid of vulnerability.
Afraid to be judged.
Afraid to be rejected.
Afraid that you won't be accepted.
It is when you stop hiding.
It is when you take your power back.
It is when you speak your truth,
That you find where you belong.
Follow your heart.
Trust in yourself.
Live in the moment.
This moment,
Right now.
This moment is now.
Walking away is hard,
But you can't carry this weight.
Set it all down.

Listen to your gut.
Leaving what you know.
Detaching from the outcome.
Letting go of any attachment.
This makes room for unconditional love.

Acceptance

Accept everything as it is.
It is what it is.
Accept people for who they are.
They are who they are.
Acceptance is a gift.
A gift you give to yourself.
A gift of love,
That you give to everyone.
A gift of love,
That you give to yourself.
Acceptance comes,
After experiencing hurt.
Hurt and pain,
Sorting through all the layers.
Layers of darkness.
Layers of suffering.
Removing the illusions.
Realizing the truth.
Seeing what's real.
Accepting it all.
Removing the stories.
Creating new beliefs.
Sitting in the void.
Crying your tears.
Feeling the loneliness.
Stop wishing for better.
Stop hoping for more.
Accept life as it is.
As it is now.
You can't be disappointed,

Without attaching to an outcome.
Detach from it all,
Suffering is gone.
Suffering comes from attachment.
Attachment to a person,
Place or thing.
Attachment to an idea.
Attachment to a purpose.
Attachment to life.
Attachment to outcomes.
Attachment to the plan.
Attachment to what you wish it could be.
Attachment to what you want it to be.
Attachment to expectations.
Release this,
And move forward.
Detach from it all,
Open your heart.
You are open for connection,
Living in auto pilot is out.
Going through the motions,
You aren't living like this.
You enjoy the present moment,
You can only be present.
This is the moment.
This moment,
Now.
Accept this truth,
Without the illusion.
Remove the future,
And what lies ahead.
Remove the outcomes,

Remove the plan.
See life as it is.
As it is now.
Accept and love.
Just love yourself.
Once you love yourself,
You can spread it to the world.

It's Okay

It's okay.
The plan has changed.
This plan was made,
In a moment.
A different moment,
That what is now.
This plan was made,
When you were someone different.
This is not who you are now.
The plan can change.
Detach from the expectation.
Detach from the outcome.
Detach from feeling guilty.
Detach from feeling shame.
Detach from the fear.
The fear you feel.
Release these feelings.
It's okay to change.
Change who you are.
Change the plan.
Change the outcome.
Change your dreams.
Change your future.
Follow your heart.
Listen to your gut.
Listen closely.
Your intuition speaks.
Get out of the noise.
Shut off the distractions.
Focus on your own voice.

What does your heart say?
Invest in yourself.
Invest in your love.
Your own self-love.
Invest in detachment.
Detaching from the plan.
Change is constant.
The only constant.
Change will come,
You must accept it.
Let go of the grudge.
This grudge you feel.
This grudge,
Holding you back.
This grudge you held.
Release it,
And be.
Be who you are.
Be who you are now.
In this moment.
This moment that comes.
There is no plan.
It's okay,
Things will change.

Authentically

When you start living authentically,
You will upset others.
You will mirror back to them,
What they can't see in themselves.
They won't like,
What they see.
You will get push back,
And people will leave.
Let them feel uncomfortable,
Let them leave.
Let them say what they want to say.
Hold space for their words,
And then let them go.
They are on their own path.
And you are on yours.
Maybe this is part of the path.
You separate from them,
So, they can go find theirs.
Their path to authenticity,
Whatever they need.
Whatever they choose,
What is best for them.
Wish them well.
Love from afar.
Sending love their way.
As you keep moving forward.
Forward on your path.
Authentic and true.
True to yourself.
Stay true to yourself.

True to your heart.
True to your soul.
Keep focused.
Don't lose yourself now.
Living authentically,
It is hard.
It can feel lonely at times...
All this letting go.
Nothing can affect you now,
On this road.
You are listening to your guide.
Your intuition,
It is so clear.
Let it guide you.
Let it lead you.
This voice is you.
This voice of clarity,
Will lead the way.
This voice of authenticity.
This authentic voice.
You know when you know.
You just know when you know.
Anything that comes,
That doesn't light you up...
Your voice will speak up,
You will use it kindly.
Kindly with love,
To communicate clearly.
Clearly and directly.
You speak up.
Your higher self.
This clarity is here,

You hear it like you never have before.
Hear it.
Listen,
In the silence.
The silence you have made.
Made for yourself,
Walking away from the noise,
Sitting in stillness.
Finding your worth,
When you do nothing at all.
Loving yourself.
Just because.
Just because you are worthy.
Worthy of it all.
Worthy of love.
Love for yourself.

The Thing You Want To Do

The thing you want to do.
Do it.
Do it now.
The dream you want,
Go get it.
Drop your fear,
This fear is not real.
This fear is an illusion.
An illusion that is here.
Grab the fear,
Bring it.
Take it with you as you walk.
The thing you want to do,
Just go do it.
Go do it now.
Achieve it.
Finish,
Make the call.
Send that email.
Just do it now.
Dive in.
Jump in.
Go all in.
That thing you want.
That thing is yours.
You know what you want,
So go get it.
The thing you want,
That thing is yours.
You have come so far,

On this path.
This path is yours,
All yours.
It is yours.
You love yourself now,
Anything goes.
You filled yourself up.
You are filled with all of your love.
You have learned to fill your cup.
Now it is time,
To set yourself free.
Go get that thing.
That thing that is yours.

Trust And Surrender

Trust in this feeling.
Trust in what's meant to be.
Surrender it all.
And just let yourself trust.
It will all work out,
Just as it's supposed to be.
It will all end up,
Just as it's supposed to.
Trust and surrender.
Surrender yourself.
Follow your heart.
Trust in yourself.
Trust in your heart beating.
Follow your heart.
Follow the lead.
The lead of your life.
Trust in the signs,
The signs that you see.
Let everything be.
Let it all just be.
Let everything go,
The way it's supposed to go,
It will play out,
Just as it's supposed to.
It will all end up,
Just as it should.
Trust and surrender.
Surrender your heart.
Believe in the plan.
This plan for you,

This plan that can't be controlled.
You can't control it,
You just have to allow.
Allow it to be.
Allow it to just be.
Whatever it is supposed to be.

Phone Calls

A phone call here.
A phone call there.
Hours and hours.
We talk about it all.
You open up.
You tell me things you have never said before.
I casually listen.
Listen to you.
I realize I love our talks.
I feel safe.
I hold this space...
This space for you.
I can listen for hours.
Hours and hours.
I hear your voice.
I listen to you.
You listen to me.
You hear what I am saying.
You understand me.
You get me.
You give your empathy.
We reach a place,
No one else knows.
No one but me.
And no one but you.
You reach a place inside of me.
A place I haven't given to anyone else.
I reach a place inside of you.
A place you haven't given to anyone else.
Just a phone call,

Here and there.
Casual and organic.
It is so easy.
So simple,
Like nothing.
We didn't plan this.
A phone call here,
And a phone there.
These phone calls,
I didn't realize.
I didn't realize what was happening.
What was happening to me.
What was happening to you.
These phone calls were organic.
They were not forced.
They lasted for hours,
With zero effort.
Effort from both of us,
We were just there.
Enjoying each other,
Over the phone.
Natural and organic.
They came from a place.
A special place that only you and I know.
These phone calls led,
To this feeling.
This feeling can't be shoved away,
Not anymore.
This feeling.
These phone calls.
This space that you are in.
This space no one has seen.

This space where no one has been.
This space in my heart.
Is where you are.
This space.
Here you are,
You are just there.

Love Is A Choice

Love is a choice.
A decision.
A conscious effort,
Of choosing over and over.
Choosing this person.
This person again.
Again and again.
Over and over.
This choice.
This love.
It is a feeling.
A feeling you will choose over and over.
This feeling you pick up.
It is a conscious choice.
This conscious effort.
This conscious choosing,
Over and over.
This feeling comes.
Let it come up.
You will keep choosing this again and again.
This love,
Can't be controlled.
Let it just be.
Let it come up.
Let it subside.
This love is a feeling.
A feeling.
A choice.
An effort.
A choosing.

A decision.
A value.
A belief.
A trust.
A loyalty.
A power.
A power over you,
That you just can't control.

Let You Be

I will leave you.
Leave you there.
Leave you in that life.
That life that you built.
I will let you go.
Let you go,
For your own good.
Actually,
For mine.
I need more than just breadcrumbs.
I will choose myself.
I will choose me,
As I let go of you.
Goodbye.
That hug.
It didn't lie.
I felt your love,
In that hug.
That hug goodbye.
That was our sign.
Leave it behind.
Leave it all behind.
Leaving you behind,
Letting go of you.
Letting go of your words.
The words that you said.
Again,
Just pretty words.
All...
Just pretty words.

Letting go of the dream.
The dream that I had,
You had it too.
Let go of you.
Let go of that wish.
Letting it be.
Let go of it.
Dropping this dream.
This dream that will never be.
Passing by each other,
In transitional times.
You are in a transition,
And so am I.
This was our sign.
Our sign of closure.
This sign of goodbye.
That hug.
Goodbye to you.
Goodbye to that wish.
That wish,
I will let go of.
This wish,
I will drop.
This dream.
This wish...
Not meant to be.
Just two people who feel,
Deeply for each other.
Just two people,
Who can't be together.
Release this wish.

Let it all go.
That's why I saw you...
To let this go.

The Lead Of Her Life

Let go of the outcomes.
Let go of the dream.
Let go of the illusions.
Let go of the what ifs.
Let go of the breadcrumbs.
The breadcrumbs of love.
Let go of the love,
That wasn't meant to be.
Let go of the dreams.
The dreams that she pictured.
Let it all flow.
Let it all play out.
Just be here.
Be here now.
Be here in this moment.
As she lets it all go.
Feel this sadness.
This sadness in her heart.
She is in this transition.
A transition for her life to start.
However long she stays here,
Is however long she needs.
Take this time to rest.
Take this time to reset.
Take this time to recharge.
She will listen to her body.
It is just her now.
Just her and her heart.
Her heart that is beating.
Her heart that is open.

She listens for her intuition.
This is her guide.
Her intuition takes the lead.
The lead of her life.

Breadcrumbs Of Love

She lived on breadcrumbs.
Breadcrumbs of love.
She lived like this,
For a very long time.
This fulfilled her.
These breadcrumbs fulfilled her.
These breadcrumbs of love,
Given to her.
She received these breadcrumbs.
These breadcrumbs of love.
She thought this was love.
Real, true love.
She lived like this,
Her whole life.
Until she stopped.
She stopped with the breadcrumbs.
These breadcrumbs of love.
She stopped receiving them.
She stopped taking them.
She walked away,
From these breadcrumbs of love.
She walked away.
Walked away,
So fast.
She gets one little glimpse.
Glimpse of a breadcrumb.
And off she goes...
Off she went.
Walking away.
Away from the breadcrumbs.

She will not receive these breadcrumbs of love.
She will not accept this anymore.
She has given up this world.
She has given up this girl.
This girl who believed.
She truly believed that words were love.
She truly believed that attention was love.
She truly believed attachment was love.
She truly believed that breadcrumbs were love.
She had no idea,
What love really was.
Manipulation and pretty words.
Validation and compliments.
Deception and betrayal,
Covered in pretty smiles and happiness.
Disrespect and lies,
Covered with facades.
Facades and masks,
That these people wore.
These people presented like they loved her.
These people pretended that they were great.
These people were putting on a façade.
These people were acting...
Acting in a play.
Acting in a show.
A show for the world,
With her as their guest.
Her as the main character.
They gave her breadcrumbs of love,
As she played her part in their show.
She played her part well,
Until she figured it out.

Until she figured out,
It was all just for show.
These breadcrumbs of love...
They were not even real.
These breadcrumbs of love,
Were all that they had.
All that they had,
Inside of them.
They didn't love themselves,
So how could they love her.
At the end of the show,
They revealed themselves.
At the end of the show,
Their masks came off.
At the end of the show,
This was all just a façade.
At the end of the show,
This illusion was shown.
At the end of the show...
These breadcrumbs of love.
These breadcrumbs of love,
Were her prize.
Standing there at the end of the show,
With her breadcrumbs of love.
This was all she had to show.
This was all she had to show,
As she gave them her all.
She gave them her all,
And all they gave her...
Were breadcrumbs of love.

This Moment Of Love

Letting go of this illusion.
Letting go of my old self.
This self,
That painted a pretty little picture.
This pretty little picture,
Made me feel safe.
This illusion,
This façade...
Made me feel safe.
This illusion,
Oh wow.
Oh my god.
I am seeing clearly now.
I see how I lived.
I see what I went through.
I can't breathe.
This illusion,
This protection.
This protection,
I had.
I had for myself,
So that I could feel numb.
I couldn't feel anything,
With this illusion.
This illusion,
Made everything good.
Everything was good,
Everything was happy.
Everything was fine,
Until it wasn't.

My life crumbled.
My life fell apart.
My whole world shattered.
My illusion fell off.
The façade.
The masks.
The rose-colored glasses.
It is a clear world now.
My eyes see clear.
This illusion is gone.
My walls are removed.
My heart is open.
I will spread love.
Removing the outcomes.
Removing the plan.
Removing the expectations.
Removing the end.
There is no end.
There is no completion.
All there is...
Is this moment.
This moment of love.

NO.

I am not here to fix you.
I am not here to be fixed.
Your problems are not my problems,
I am done taking them on.
I will speak my truth,
Even if it's not good for you.
I will use my voice,
Because that's what is best for me.
I am done doing,
What is good for everyone else.
Everyone else,
Except for myself.
I will do what's best for me.
I will choose myself.
I choose me.
Your problems are not my problems,
Stop guilt tripping me.
Stop with the excuses,
And just admit.
Admit that you have problems.
These problems are yours.
These problems are not mine,
I will give them back to you.
I will not be scolded ever again...
For doing what is best for me.
I will not be punished ever again...
For not being at your beckon call.
I will stop being the nice one...
Always the nice one.
I will stop being manipulated,

And playing your game.
NO.
I will stop being the one,
To always sacrifice myself.
I will stop being the one,
To forgive everyone.
I am good at forgiving,
But not when I am consistently walked on.
Walked on.
Walked over.
Brutally disrespected.
NO.
It is my turn now.
I have had enough.
If you try to put your problems on me,
I will give them back to you….
Kindly with love,
They all go back to you.
I will walk away so fast,
You won't even know what hit you.
NO.
I am not your doormat.
I am not your backpack.
Your backpack,
To carry every single problem you have.
I am not your object,
That you can pick up and put down.
I am not the ground that you walk on.
NO.
I am done.
Walking away.
I will stand up for myself,

No matter what now.
I will never allow this behavior ever again.
NO.
This is not okay,
To use humans this way.
NO.
I am done being disrespected.
I am done with the games.
I am done with the betrayal.
I am done with you using me,
To meet your needs.
NO.
I am a person.
I have a heart.
A heart of gold,
That I share with mostly everyone.
I wear my heart on my sleeve...
Maybe that's wrong.
But the ones who treat it with care...
Those are the ones,
Standing with me now.
These are the ones,
Who respect my heart.
Thank you for being the ones,
Who respect me...
No matter what.
I am worth more than being the ground.
The ground that you stand on.
The ground that you stomp on.
I am done being that one.
NO.
I am done being the girl,

That you use to dump on.
I am done being the girl,
Who is at everyone's beckon call.
I am done being the girl,
Who worries about everyone else...
Putting myself aside,
Every single time.
I do it out of love.
Because of my heart.
My heart is so big,
And I always find understanding.
I try to understand each and every person,
In my life.
But I am done being the only one who does this,
Every time.
I am done being used.
Used to meet every need you have.
I am done being chosen,
When it is good for you.
Always on your terms,
Never on mine.
I will speak up...
Say words that you don't want to hear.
Say truthful words,
Genuine words...
Words that aren't meant to make you smile.
My words out of my mouth,
Will be truthful and honest.
And it doesn't matter to me anymore,
If you don't like my words.
I will not sugar coat.
I will not be controlled.

I will use my words,
Assertively...
To stand up for myself.
It's been too many times.
Too many times,
Of blatant disrespect.
I deserve more...
More than this.
I deserve to be treated with love.
I deserve to be handled with care.
I deserve to be treated with respect.
I deserve to be seen and heard.
I deserve to be seen for who I am.
Who am I?
A girl with so much love to give.
Love that I give away,
Unconditionally.
Love that I have for you,
That you take advantage of.
And then I am the one...
Sitting here hurt.
Sitting here worried.
Sitting here analyzing what happened.
Sitting here,
With all of your problems.
NO.
It is time for me now.
It is time for my voice now.
If you even try to put your problems on me now,
I will speak my truth now...
And give your problems back.
Walking away and not looking back.

Your New Life Will Cost You

Your new life will cost you.
Cost you,
Everything you have.
Everything you loved.
Everything you built.
Everything you knew.
Your new life will cost you.
Cost you your old life.
Walking away from everything you know.
Accepting everything as it is...
Everyone for who they are.
Setting boundaries,
To protect yourself.
Walking away,
From anything that is not yours.
Anything that brings you misery.
Anything that brings you anxiety.
Anything that brings you down.
Anyone who doesn't see you for you.
Anyone who is using you.
Walking away,
From meeting everyone's needs.
Walking away,
From everything.
Nothing else matters...
Except for you.
How are you feeling?
Are you staying true?
True to yourself?
Are you being you?

Anyone that won't allow you to be you,
Those are not your people.
Time to say goodbye.
Anyone who doesn't respect you for you,
Those are not your people.
Time to walk away,
You are done fixing problems.
Problems that are not yours.
Not yours to solve,
They are not yours to touch.
You are done giving the second chance,
Because you feel bad.
Feel bad for them.
Finding forgiveness always,
For their poor actions.
You are done with false hope.
You are done with the illusion.
Everything is as it is...
Stop with the wishing.
Let everything be.
Let everything go.
Other people are not your problem,
Their problems are not yours.
Drop the relationship,
If it's not nurturing your soul.
Drop the constant giving,
If it is not genuine.
Genuine love,
Is what you give.
Authenticity is your place now.
Authentic giving.
Authentic love.

Unconditional...
No matter what.
But make sure to protect your heart.
Make sure you are surrounded,
With people who make you feel safe.
Feel safe and protected.
Who also give to just give.
They want nothing in return.
They are not using you,
For their own gain.
They are also genuine.
Those lessons,
You carry.
You carry them closely.
You hold them,
And know when it is a lesson.
You listen closely.
You follow the signs.
You are in full surrender.
Trust in the process.
Your new life will cost you.
Cost you it all.
Cost you everything...
Everything in your old life.

Not My Mess

This is not my mess.
My mess to clean up.
Why am I always cleaning up everyone's mess?
This is not my mess.
I did not make it.
Why am I the one cleaning it up?
This is not my mess.
I did not make it.
Why am I the one cleaning it up?
This is not my mess.
I did not make it.
Why are you expecting me,
To clean up your mess?
Oh,
Because of my heart?
Because I am the giver?
Because I take the blame?
Because I am the fixer?
Because I feel bad for you?
Yeah, no thanks.
Not my mess.
Done cleaning it up.
This is your mess.
Your mess that you made.
You are to blame.
Quit pointing the finger,
The finger at me.
Why are you pointing?
Pointing your finger?
Is it because you know...

That you made this mess?
Deep down you know...
And you feel shame,
This is not my problem.
I am not the one to blame.
This mess is not mine.
I will not clean it up.
Not this time,
Not in the future.
This mess is yours.
You made this mess.
The accountability is yours.
This responsibility you are not taking,
Has me shocked.
Shocked in awe.
That I did not see this until now.
These messes I have been cleaning.
Cleaning them up.
Cleaning up messes,
That were never mine to begin with.
This mess is yours.
Accept this truth.
This is your mess.
This is on you.
I am done taking the blame.
I am done feeling this anxiety.
This anxiety about this mess.
Your mess,
Not mine.
Time to clean it up.
Get your act together.
This mess is waiting to be picked up.

And I will not be standing there at the end.
Because I gave you chance after chance.
And still you proved.
Proved in action,
Every single time.
Proving it still.
Still to this day.
Standing over this mess,
You are the one to blame.
Still not taking accountability.
Using your pretty words.
Your pretty words are all you have,
Because your insides are bare.
Because you live disconnected.
Disconnected from yourself.
This is why you are making this mess.
Mess after mess.
Because you are disconnected from your heart.
Not my problem.
My problem to fix.
I am not showing.
Showing you how.
I have worked on my insides.
I have worked so hard on them,
That I need to be done cleaning up your mess.

I Am Not A Possession

I am a person.
I am not your possession.
I am a real person.
I can make my own choices.
I can do what I want to do,
It is not up to you.
It is not up to you,
To make my decisions.
My problems are mine,
They are not yours.
They are mine to deal with,
It is not up to you.
It is not up to you,
To fix them for me.
I am not your possession,
I am a real person.
I can make choices,
That benefit me.
The way I live my life,
Has nothing to do with you.
The way I decide to go,
Has nothing to do with you.
When I take space,
It is not about you.
When I do my own thing,
It is not about you.
So why every time...
Do you make it about you?
My life is about me,
Not about you.

If I want to change,
That's what I can do.
The people who support me...
During these changes.
These are my people,
I am thankful for them.
I am not their possession.
They let me be my own person,
Without making it about them.
They just let me do my thing.
I am not a possession.
I am me.
I realized this,
When I took the time.
When I took the time to give love to myself.
I am not a possession,
I will not be treated like one.
I don't belong to anyone...
I belong to me.

I Am Not Here...

I am not an object.
An object to use.
I am not a tool,
A tool for your life.
I am not here,
To serve your every need.
I am not here,
To be at your beckon call.
I am not here,
To be put down and abused.
I am not here,
To play a game with you.
I am not here,
To meet all of your needs.
The needs you can't meet for yourself.
The needs that you ignore.
I am not here,
To take on your problems.
I am not here,
To be the fixer of your issues.
I am not here,
To be your punching bag.
I am not here,
To be completely dismissed.
I am not here,
To be unconsidered.
I am not here,
To be the constant lifter.
I am not here,
To be your therapist.

I am not here,
To meet your every need.
I am not here,
To serve a purpose for you.
I am not here,
To give you everything you want.
This is not how life works.
This is not how *my* life works.
I have done this for far too long.
Living for everyone else.
I have done this for many years.
Being at everyone's beckon call.
I am a loyal person.
I will give you so much love.
I will be there to lift you up.
I will be there to support you.
But I can't be that person,
If I don't take care of myself.
I cannot be that person,
If I don't give myself love.
I cannot be that person,
If I do not heal myself.
I cannot be that person,
If I don't fill myself up.
I cannot be that person,
If I don't take the rest that I need.
I cannot be that person,
If I don't recharge my battery.
I cannot be that person,
If I don't start standing up for myself.
Defending myself,
From being walked on and used.

Defending myself,
From your manipulative words.
I will stand up for myself now,
No matter what.
Standing up for myself,
Is how I give myself love.

Love Just Is

She realized when,
She loved herself...
When she put the illusion down.
The illusion of what she knew.
That love doesn't have to be proven.
Love is not a transaction.
Love just is.
Love is a choice,
Both for her and for him.
Love is easy,
Love feels good.
Love is not a test.
Healthy love heals.
Healthy love soothes.
It's like love for herself,
The love feels smooth.
Love is not two hearts,
That are closed off.
Love is two hearts,
That are open.
Love is two hearts,
Open to receive.
Love is two hearts,
That can both give.
Love is two hearts,
That are connected.
Love is two hearts,
That beat together.
Not as one,
But separate.

Love is two hearts,
That can beat without the other.
Love is two hearts that stand,
Side by side.
Love is two hearts,
That are completely in sync.
Love is partnership.
Love is understanding.
Love is not a game.
The games come from wounds.
Love casts out fear.
Love comes from healing.
Love is learning.
Love comes when,
Two people are whole.
Love is patient.
Love is kind.
Love is trust.
Love is honest.
Love is emotional maturity.
Love is self-awareness.
Love is conscious.
Love is faith.
Love is when,
Two people,
Love themselves.
Love themselves,
Completely.
Love themselves,
First.
Love is growth.
And then those two people,

Come together.
And ignite a flame,
So powerful...
It will never go out.
That flame is love.
She is not going to settle,
She will say no to the games.
She will wait on that flame.
And if that flame never comes,
At least she is lucky enough,
To have found love in herself.

This Love That I Seek

This love that I seek.
This love that is in me,
This love that I found.
My very own love.
I found my heart.
This love that I seek.
It will match me,
Match what is inside.
Inside of me.
Unconditional love.
This love that I seek,
It will be pure.
It will be equal.
It will be balanced.
It will not be for gain.
On either part.
Love is not gain.
Love is a flow.
Up and down.
Give and take.
Love is not for gain.
Love is not for show.
Love is love.
Love comes from the heart.
This love that I seek,
Will match me.
This love in me,
This love that I found.
This love is unconditional.
Unconditional love.

Love can hurt.
Love is tender.
Love can be pain.
Love can be waiting.
Waiting with patience.
Just let love be.
Whatever it is.
Unconditional love.
This is what I give.
I will love you,
From a distance.
I will love you,
Even if I had to let go.
I send you my love,
If you are not around.
I will send you love,
No matter what.
Love is just there.
Love is in the air.
Love is a flow.
Up and down.
Sometimes it's more.
Sometimes it's less.
Love will be rocky.
Love will dim out.
Dim out if you don't nurture it.
Nurture your love.
Love will be picked up.
Picked up again and again.
Love is a choice.
Love is an action.
An action you choose.

Choose it over and over.
Over and over,
Again and again.
Love is a flow.
Up and down.
Sometimes it burns.
Sometimes it feels good.
Sometimes it is confusing.
Sometimes it is certain.
Sometimes it doesn't make sense.
Sometimes it makes perfect sense.
Love is a flame,
That can't be burned out.
This constant flame.
Love is fire.
Just sit back,
And let love be.
Let love be,
Whatever it wants to be.
Love is here.
Love is in me.
Love is flowing.
Flowing in me.
My love is light.
This light that shines.
Shines so bright.
My light I hold.
I hold it close.
Close to my heart.
My light I found.
I found in my love.
Love for myself.
My love is my light.

Signs

I ask for signs.
I look for signs.
Signs that are there.
Signs to tell me.
Tell me answers.
Answers to my questions.
Tell me what is right,
And which way to go.
Signs to guide me.
Signs to lead me.
This sign comes.
Comes as a test.
To test myself.
To test my mind.
To test my heart.
To test my life.
This sign may come.
Come as a lesson.
A lesson for me.
For me to learn.
This sign comes.
Comes to tell me.
Tell me that I am going the right way.
This sign comes,
To bring me comfort.
This sign comes,
Because this is what I need.
What I need in this moment.
This sign comes.
Comes to show me what is right.
What is right for me.

What is right,
Right now.
This sign comes,
To show me forgiveness.
To show me forgiveness,
To release this weight.
This weight,
That is in me.
This weight that I carry.
This resentment that I carry.
Carry around.
I have been carrying it,
All this time.
This sign comes,
To give me what I need.
Exactly what I need,
At the exact time that I need it.
Bring me my signs.
Show them to me.
I will trust in them always.
They are here for me to see,
To pay attention.
To give me guidance.
Send me my signs.
Keep them coming.
These signs are for me,
On my journey.

Hold My Emotions

If you cannot hold my emotions,
Hold them with me.
Then you don't have to be here,
You can leave.
If you cannot stand the chaos.
The chaos of emotions.
You don't have to hold them.
Hold them with me.
My emotions are strong.
They are here.
If you cannot hold them,
Hold them with me.
Then you don't have to be here.
You have freedom to leave.
If my emotions make you uncomfortable,
That's okay.
You have emotions too.
But if you cannot hold yours,
And you want to throw them onto me...
That is not okay.
I will not stay.
You have emotions.
Your emotions are yours.
Yours to feel.
Not yours to throw onto others,
Or project onto me.
Feel your emotions,
And I will help hold them.
But I can't help you hold them,
If you are throwing them around.

Throwing them onto everyone else.
Throwing them at me,
So that you don't have to feel.
Oh,
No.
I will not stay.
Your emotions are yours.
They are yours to feel.
Please stop throwing them at everyone else.
My emotions are mine,
They are mine to feel.
They are mine to hold.
And you can help hold them too.
Your emotions are yours.
They are yours to feel.
They are yours to hold.
And I can help hold them too.
We can do this together.
This brings vulnerability.
This is real, true intimacy.
Bring your self-awareness.
Bring it with you.
Be in your body,
Let yourself feel.
You will need to understand your body.
You will need to understand your awareness,
To understand all of your emotions.

This Platter

She sees things differently.
Differently than others.
She sees what is real.
She sees the truth.
She will call it out.
This disfunction,
She sees.
This insanity,
She knows.
She knows it well.
She knows this truth.
This truth,
She tells.
This façade falls off.
This illusion is revealed.
It all comes unraveled.
The silver platter has been put down.
This pretty, silver platter.
This platter,
She carried.
Those pretty words are now the truth.
Those pretty words have faded away.
The words she speaks are no longer pretty.
The words she speaks are blatant truth.
The words she speaks are reality.
Reality that you don't want to hear.
Reality that disturbs your illusion.
Reality that disturbs your peace.
Reality that disturbs your façade.
This façade that you put on.

This façade.
This mask.
It is all disturbed.
Disturbed and crushed.
The façade is messed up.
She messed this up.
Messed this up for you.
You no longer like her,
Or want to be around her.
Because she doesn't play along.
She is not playing along.
Along with your façade.
She is not playing along.
Along with the chaos.
Her silver platter she has put down.
Her pretty, silver platter,
That she has carried.
She has put it down for good.
She will no longer serve you.
Serve what you need.
She will no longer serve you,
To keep you on your pedestal.
She will no longer serve you,
And be at your beckon call.
She will no longer serve you.
Serve you with her energy.
Her beautiful, peaceful energy.
That she used to give away.
Served on a silver platter,
For anyone that came.
Anyone that came.
Came her way.

Here you go,
On this platter.
This platter is all yours.
This platter she served.
She served your every need.
Anything you want.
Anything you need.
It was all out on this platter,
And served to you.
Just the way you like it.
Just the perfect way.
Just to make you comfortable.
This was her role.
Her role to serve you.
Serve you with this platter.
This platter was filled.
Filled with what worked for you.
Whatever worked for you.
Whatever you needed.
She was there serving this platter.
This platter has been put down.
She will no longer be serving.
Serving you pretty words.
Serving you with validation.
Validation that you need.
You need this validation,
To feel fulfilled.
You need this validation,
So that you feel loved.
She has put this platter down,
Because she has figured this out.
She now deserves this platter,

More than anyone else.
She is now serving herself.
Herself,
This beautiful platter.
Everything she needs is on this platter.
Her needs.
Her energy.
Her worth.
Her love.
This all comes on her platter.
This platter that is now her own.
This platter is now hers.
Hers to serve.
Serve to herself.
This platter of self-love.

Pretty Little Thing

When I stopped being his pretty little thing...
His pretty little thing that sits in his car.
His pretty little thing that stands by his side.
His pretty little object.
His object, that is his.
His pretty little plaything,
That he gives transactional love.
"If you do this for me,
I will do this for you."
This is what he really said to me.
"You don't even cook or clean for me."
He said this too.
When he stood over me and looked me in my eyes,
During a moment of love.
"Yeah, I'm all set with this, I'm good."
Stood up over me,
Looking down over me.
This condescending behavior,
Was getting to be too much for me.
I was his pretty little thing.
That he could pick up and put down.
His pretty little thing that he could show off.
If I acted a certain way.
A certain way for him.
It was always about him,
Even when I was sick.
He used to talk about how he *used to be* a narcissist.
Oh... but not anymore...
Whenever I would use my voice.
Share my feelings.

Say what he did not want to hear,
It would end in a fight.
These inappropriate reactions...
It was all about him.
I made a request.
Can you please stop hanging out with a girl,
That you slept with?
She is always around,
And this feels weird.
She would come to see his dog...
A rage came out.
This rage in him.
His answer was no,
Not a chance.
He told me this is okay...
He's okay with it,
Because, why would my feelings matter?
He is in control,
And he will have this girl.
Have this girl around,
Because this suited him.
He would shut my voice down,
Shut it down so fast.
And then he'd start handing out,
The put downs.
The put downs were for me.
The put downs were his compliments.
Put me down,
Subtly of course.
"What?!"
It was just a joke."
He used to announce,

When he would do something nice.
He used to announce,
That he was a good guy.
He used to have sayings hanging up on his wall...
How he was a man of integrity.
He would stand tall,
While announcing this all.
He is a stand-up guy.
A stand-up guy,
With a pretty little thing.
A stand-up guy,
Who would put the blame on me.
We had a friendship first.
A friendship that was not genuine.
A friendship that was built,
With conditions and transactions.
He showed me this from the very beginning.
But I couldn't see this.
See this at first.
I couldn't see this,
Because this is how I was raised.
This appeared normal.
Normal to me.
Transactional love.
I was always proving my love.
If I do this for them,
Maybe they will love me...
Love me unconditionally.
That's all I ever wanted.
It was...
"If you do this for me,
I will do this for you."

Let me put in a transaction,
So that they won't leave.
Let me put in a transaction,
So that they will stay.
Let me put in a transaction,
So that they feel loved.
Let me give you my all.
This transactional love.
"She must behave this way,
She must not speak up.
She must not speak the truth…"
Well guess what, I am now.
I am speaking my truth.
Because I am not your thing.
I am not a possession with a turn off switch.
Turn me on and turn me off.
I am not your thing,
That you can throw away.
I am not your thing,
That you can control and use.
I am not your thing,
That you use to feel good.
I am not your thing…
That you can walk on,
And use as your punching bag.
I am not your thing,
That you use for a transaction.
You got what you wanted,
So, you can leave.
You didn't hear what you wanted,
So, you never return.
As soon as I returned home to myself.

As soon as I figured all of this out.
As soon as I opened my eyes.
As soon as I started to speak the truth.
As soon as I started standing my ground.
As soon as I started defending myself.
As soon as I took my power back.
The people who were using me,
They all left...
And didn't return.
They all left,
When I spoke my truth.
They all disappeared and did not return.
I stopped giving them their transactions.
Their transactional love.
Their love on a silver platter,
That I delivered.
Delivered by me,
This transactional love.
Let me bring you this love,
On a pretty, little platter.
I am not your pretty, little thing.
I am not an object.
An object to use.
I am a person.
I have feelings.
I have a heart.
I am putting this platter down.
This pretty, little platter...
With all of my love.
It is time now,
To speak my truth.

She Is Done With Transactional Love

They were there,
When she needed them.
They were there,
Each time she called.
They were there,
They came running.
Running to her,
Each time she asked.
They were there for her,
When she needed them the most.
She will say thank you to them.
Thank you for this.
This was not enough,
They needed more.
Hearing the words thank you,
Is just not enough.
These things they did.
They did for her.
This was all thrown back in her face.
They threw it back,
Right back in her face.
They threw it all right back.
Back in her face.
They didn't do this out of love.
They didn't do this out of the kindness in their hearts.
They didn't do this out of a genuine place.
Because why are they throwing this back in her face?
Yes, they were there.
Yes, they came to her rescue.
But did they do it for them?

Did they do it because they genuinely care?
Or did they do this to hold it over her head?
"We did all of this.
All of this for you.
We have done so much for you."
Please don't say this.
Say this to her.
She has never said this once.
Never once has she done something,
For someone else...
Those words have never come out of her mouth.
They never will...
Because when she does something for someone else,
She will not expect anything in return.
She does it out of love.
Pure unconditional love.
This is all she has ever wanted.
To be loved unconditionally.
"Please love me,
Without conditions.
Please love me,
When I don't put in a transaction.
Please love me,
When I have nothing to give.
Please just love me,
When I'm kicked down to the ground.
Please just love me,
When I am at my lowest.
Please just love me,
Even though I have changed."
But this transactional love...
This does not work this way.

We will do this for you,
But you must then give something in return.
You must always contribute.
You must always give back.
You must act this way,
For us to give anything to you.
You must say the right words...
And not argue back.
You must not disagree,
Or take care of yourself.
You must not have any boundaries.
You must do as you are told.
We will come to help you,
But then you must help us.
We will take care of you,
But in the way that we choose.
You must not be yourself.
You must not live your own life.
You must be an extension of us.
You must not make a mistake.
You must not even get sick.
And if you do...
We will find a punishment for you.
We will take our love away.
We will pout in the corner,
Because we did not get our way.
It is up to you,
To meet our needs.
And if you don't,
We will throw it back in your face.
This is your job,
To meet our needs.

Your job,
Is to never change.
Do not ever change,
Into whom you want to be.
You must not become the person,
You were always meant to be.
You are just simply not worthy.
This is when she took her power back.
She will never again put her worth,
In someone else's hands.
She will never again make herself small.
She will never again fall for transactional love.
She will walk away the very first minute.
That very first minute,
She gets a glimpse of transactional love.
No, thank you.
She is done.
She is walking away.
It is confirmed...
She is done,
With transactional love.

Weapon Of Destruction

Withholding love.
This is what she knows.
This is what is familiar.
Familiar to her.
Love will be taken away.
Taken away if you change.
Love will be withheld.
Withheld if you act out.
Love will be taken.
Taken away from her.
Love has been used as a weapon.
This weapon of destruction.
This weapon has kept her small.
This weapon has kept her.
Kept her from what she loved.
This weapon.
This withholding of love.
Take all the love away.
She is not who we want her to be.
Stop with the acts of love.
She uses words we don't want to hear.
Take away that love,
We will disappear.
She stands up for herself.
She gets love taken from her.
She is not worthy,
Worthy of our love.
She doesn't do what we want her to do,
We are in control.
Control of this love.

This love that we give.
She will be punished.
Punished with this weapon.
This weapon that we control.
This weapon that we use.
This love that she depends on.
We will take it all away.
Take it away until there is nothing left.
Nothing left for her.
This was her biggest gift.
This weapon of destruction.
Because of having love taken from her.
Taken from her,
Her whole life.
This left her to fend for herself.
This left her to find her very own love.
This love inside of herself.
And once she found this love.
This love inside of herself...
This weapon couldn't affect her.
Couldn't affect her anymore.
This withholding...
The giving and the taking away.
The acts of love withdrawn from her.
This game that she played,
Chasing love.
Chasing love,
To feel filled up.
This weapon of destruction.
This no longer worked.
Worked on her.
Because of this love that she found.

This love that she found was her very own light.
Her light that could not be dimmed.
Dimmed from the outside.
Dimmed from this weapon.
Dimmed from a punishment.
Dimmed from abuse.
Because now she knows.
She knows the truth.
The truth that she discovered.
This withholding of love...
This never had anything to do with her.
This tactic.
This weapon.
This had to do with them.
This was their way of survival,
And had nothing to do with her.
She stopped putting her worth,
Into the palms of their hands.
She started to hold her worth,
In her palm.
In her palm of her hand.
She discovered this truth,
As she found her light.
This light is her love.
This light is her gift.
This gift, that came from transactional love.

The Villain

She will be the villain.
The villain in your story.
That is what she has always been.
This villain in your story.
She has accepted that this is what she will always be.
She will be the villain.
This villain in your story.
Because this is how you must live.
This is what makes you feel better.
This is what brings you comfort.
It is okay...
She has accepted this.
You need to paint this picture.
This picture of her,
To cover up the truth.
You must live in denial,
So that you can't see the damage that you have done.
You need to paint this picture,
So that you don't see yourself.
You paint this picture of her.
This villain of your story.
You do this to protect yourself,
From feeling anything inside.
You do this because it is easier to blame someone else.
You do this to avoid accountability.
You do this to avoid any responsibility.
This villain of your story...
She will accept this role.
She knows what really went on.
And she knows the truth.

She understands now...
That in order for her to move on,
She must be the villain in your story.
She will not defend herself,
She will just walk away.
Walk away from it all...
Because why stay?
There is no point anymore.
Nothing will ever change.
She put her time in,
Trying to change this disfunction.
This disfunction she couldn't live in.
She put her time in,
To put an end to all of this.
She put her time in,
Trying to prove herself.
She put her time in,
Trying to give you all of her love.
She put her time in,
Trying to prove her worth to you.
She just needed to see,
That this was the disfunction.
She played a role.
She played a part.
She stopped with all the efforts,
When she realized that this will never change.
She finally reached acceptance.
Acceptance that this is the way it is.
She walked away knowing that she will be,
The villain.
The villain of your story.

Living My Life

No to this.
No to that.
This is not for me.
Neither is this.
You are not my person.
No, this is not working.
No, this is not the thing.
The thing for me.
No, I can feel...
Something is off.
This is not for my life.
No, this is not me.
People say I am too picky.
But I know myself well.
I have been picked up and put down,
So many times.
It has been me to pick myself back up.
Back up when I've been kicked down.
Every single time that I get kicked down,
It is me that figures out how to get back up.
So,
Yes.
I am picky.
Yes, I say no a lot.
Yes,
I walk away.
Walk away from anything.
Anything that is not for me.
And I know myself well.
Well enough.

Well enough to know what I like,
And what I don't.
I have been picking myself up.
Picking myself back up all these years.
So yes,
I know how I like to feel.
I know myself well.
I know what I like.
I know what I don't.
There is really no middle ground.
It is either I know,
Or I don't.
When I don't really know,
And I need to figure it out...
I give myself a little bit of time.
And then I say yes.
Or It is a no.
I can recognize transactional love.
I recognize it pretty quickly now,
And it is a no to that.
I can recognize now,
If you are using me.
I see it faster than I used to,
And I will walk away from that too.
I notice those put downs.
I notice your pretty words.
Those pretty words that have no action.
I recognize this now too.
The illusion I had...
It is gone.
I see for real now,
What is really going on.

I won't be your distraction.
I won't be your project.
I won't be your object.
I won't be your fill in.
I won't stand there,
So that you feel good.
I won't put up with your punishments.
The punishments you give me.
People say I'm too picky.
People like to criticize me.
But guess what...
That's okay.
Those are your projections.
Your projections of me.
Because if you knew anything about me...
You would know how well I know myself.
You would also know that I have been through a lot.
Going through all of the downs,
Leaves me to know myself so well.
Leaves me to figure out what will work,
And what won't.
People say I'm too picky.
And that's okay.
I will be too picky,
It is up to me.
Up to me to decide.
Decide who comes in.
Who comes with me,
And who doesn't.
This is my life,
And I can choose.
I can choose who stays.

I can choose who goes.
Please do not pull me down,
Just let me be.
This is my life.
My life now.
I am finally living my life.
Living my life for me.

I Used to...

I used to think my purpose was,
To meet everyone else's needs.
I used to think my purpose was,
To please everyone else.
I used to think my purpose was,
To keep everyone else happy.
I used to think my purpose was,
To fix everyone's problems.
I used to think this.
I really believed this.
But now,
I realize my purpose is me.
Live my life the way I choose.
While still spreading love from me to you.
I can love you and myself.
I can love everyone else,
While still loving myself.
I can still spread love,
Without sacrificing myself.
Without abandoning myself,
Until I have nothing left.
I will meet my needs,
Before I meet yours.
And now I believe,
How worthy I am.
I will not be scolded for not meeting your needs.
I will not be punished.
I will not be torn down.
My purpose is more.
More than just meeting your needs.

I am here to live and love,
And to be loved too.
Not to be used.
I will not be walked on.
And if that means not being liked,
Then I am okay with that.
I don't need to be liked.
And I certainly don't need to be used.
I will walk away,
From anything that's not mine.
I will walk away,
From people who bring me down.
I will just walk away.
No more explaining.
No more over giving.
I will just stop giving you, my energy.
I deserve more.
I have a huge heart.
A heart that I gave out to everyone else.
I would understand when you needed help.
I would see where it came from.
I would always understand.
But I am done...
Those are your problems,
Not mine.
And when you have a problem,
And you put them on me...
When you put expectations on me...
I am just done.
I will still send you love.
Send you love from afar.
Send you love from a distance.

I am a real person.
And it is now time,
To live my life.

Me

If you are coming at me.
Coming at me with your shit.
If you are coming at me.
Coming at me bringing problems.
If you are coming at me...
Coming at me with a script.
A script you expect me to follow.
If you are coming at me,
While you are unaware.
Please step back.
Step back from me.
Your unawareness is affecting me,
It is affecting my energy.
Please wake up.
Please be aware.
Unaware people,
Please stay away.
I am done being the fixer.
I am done being your lifter.
I am done being the one,
To always step up.
I am done being the one,
Who is expected to follow your script.
Your rules and regulations,
That you give me to follow.
You have me on this leash,
And I am breaking free.
Free of this leash.
I will not be controlled.
I will not be expected,

To be who you expect me to be.
I am me.
That is who I am,
And I am done not being seen for me.
I am me,
And I am worthy.
I am me,
And I see me finally.
I am me...
This is me.

Underneath

We live in a world,
Where people do not feel feelings.
People do not go inside.
Inside of themselves.
People do not challenge.
Challenge what they know.
Challenge their world.
Challenge their beliefs.
Beliefs that are engrained.
Engrained in them.
People do not challenge.
Challenge the illusion.
This illusion they have lived in.
Because they think that is who they are.
This is just what they know.
They see through eyes...
Eyes that are fogged.
Fogged with the illusion.
The illusion of what they know.
The illusions of what they've been taught.
The illusion of what they love.
Society's beliefs.
Society's illusion.
We live in a world.
This world of instant gratification.
Everything is fixed,
Immediately.
Everything is fixed,
Externally.
Family and generational beliefs.

What they are raised in.
Their family's ways.
How they were brought up,
What they saw.
This brings an illusion.
An illusion they know.
It is what they know.
It is what they've seen.
Everything is aligned.
Aligned by this illusion.
But what if you knock this illusion down?
Get rid of this illusion.
Underneath this illusion.
Underneath all of these layers...
This is where you find the truth.

Loud and Clear

I hear my soul.
Loud and clear.
On a day like today.
Laying on the grass,
I hear my soul.
I am connected.
Connected to myself.
Connected to myself,
More than ever before.
I hear my soul,
Loud and clear.
I am connected.
Connected to my soul.
I hear my soul.
I hear my voice.
I hear my intuition.
My intuition speaks.
My intuition guides me,
My intuition leads me.
My intuition gives me answers,
That I can only hear in silence.
My voice I hear,
Loud and clear.
My soul I feel.
It is loud and clear.
I have answers.
Answers to lead me.
Lead me to where I have to go.
Where I have to go,
To fulfil my soul.
I hear this today,

On this beautiful day.
My hair is blowing.
I am free.
I am free from society's beliefs.
I am free.
Freer than ever.
There are no rules.
Rules for me.
I will follow my light,
As I let everything go.
All that I know...
Except for my soul.
I will carry my love.
I will hold it close.
I will hear my voice.
Loud and clear.
As I connect with nature,
This is all I hear.
My intuition,
Connected to my soul.
Breathe in.
Breathe out.
Here I am.
Nothing to do.
Nowhere to go.
I will hear my intuition.
I will let it lead the way.
I hear it in silence,
Away from the noise.
I am connected.
I cannot ignore it.
Here it is,
Loud and clear.

Room to Bloom.

The people who stand by you.
The people who stay.
Stay the whole time.
Stay and stand with you.
The people who stand with you.
Stand with you,
At your side.
The people who are standing.
Standing with you at the end.
As they stand with you,
As you find yourself.
As you rediscover who you are,
After you lost yourself.
Lost the pieces,
That made up who you are.
Picking up the pieces,
All by yourself.
Moving through all the layers,
As you find your true self.
The people who support you,
While you figure it all out.
The people who just let you be.
Let you hang out.
Hang out with yourself.
The people who still give you love along the way.
Along the road.
Along your journey,
Without expecting anything in return.
The people who just let you go.
Let you be you.

The people who don't scold you,
For the decisions you make.
The people who don't question your distance,
Wondering where you went.
Other people,
Making it all about them.
You stood by them,
This whole time.
Supporting their life...
You let them go be them...
You allowed them to be them.
You allowed them to build their life.
You loved watching them build their life.
It was beautiful to you,
To watch them build their life.
Some things aren't meant to last forever.
Everything comes,
Everything goes.
When it was your turn...
To become who you were meant to be...
Some people left.
And this is okay.
Some you had to leave,
You had to walk away.
This is a lesson,
You had to learn.
A lesson that came,
Along the way.
Those aren't your people.
You made space for your people,
Along the way.
Along your path,

On your journey.
Letting go of the old,
Making room for new.
Making room for fresh.
Making room to bloom.
Find your people.
Make space to be you.
Speak your truth,
As you become you.

She Found Freedom

(She found freedom.
Freedom with her voice.
Freedom in her words.
The words that she speaks.)
For so many years,
Being told to, not to say a word.
Staying in freeze mode,
Or being told to, not say a word.
Do not open your mouth.
Do not use your voice and do what you are told.
If you do use your voice,
We will abandon you.
Punish you.
Scold you.
Gaslight you,
And demean you.
Dismiss you,
Or turn it around...
To make it about us.
It is all about us.
And what we want.
What is good for us.
What works for us.
It is not about you.
Only we matter.
Your feelings don't.
Do not say a word.
Do not use your voice.
You must stay silent,
And do as you are told.

You are not allowed to change,
Or we will scold you.
Instead of allowing you to be,
Whoever you want to be.
Instead of allowing you to go,
Wherever you want to go.
We will control you.
You are a possession.
A possession to our life.
 We will never take the time,
To understand you.
We will make it about us.
We will pout because we didn't get our way.
We will be hurt,
Because we heard words that we didn't want to hear.
We are not open to learn,
Or to understand.
We won't give our empathy,
Not to you.
We don't want to learn this new you,
That you have found.
This is too much work for us,
To learn a new way.
We will use you,
To meet our needs.
We will put expectations on you.
We will expect you to be your best.
We will expect you to give your all.
We will expect you to keep your mouth shut,
While you are meeting our needs.
...and when you do call this out...
When you do use your voice.

When you do speak your truth…
We will scold you.
We will become defensive,
And yell at you.
Say mean words to hurt you,
Because we are emotionally immature.
We want things our way,
And now you are taking your power back.
Power away from us.
Power that we had.
Power over you.
We had the power.
(She let them have power,
This was on her.
This was her mistake,
For never speaking up.
She allowed this,
This was on her.
She allowed this to go on for far too long.)
When you take your power back,
We will abandon you.
Abandon our relationship.
Because your communication is different.
Your communication has changed.
You speak in a way,
That we have never heard before.
We do not like this new voice.
We do not like this new way.
We have never heard you talk this way.
We have never heard your voice.
We have never seen you show emotion,
Because you shoved it so deeply down.

This truth that you speak now,
We don't want to hear.
Your voice that you use,
Fills us with fear.
(The truth that she speaks now,
This is her freedom.
This is her way out.
Her way out of this cage.
Her voice.
Her truth.
This is her freedom.
Her freedom she found.
She found in her love.
Inside of her love,
That she found for herself.)

Light, Like A Feather

She became light.
Light, like a feather.
She became lighter.
Lighter than ever.
She put the weight down.
All of the weight.
She emptied it out.
She stopped carrying it.
She became light,
Just like a feather.
She became free.
Free,
Like a bird.
She dropped the weight.
This weight that was weighing her down.
She became light.
So light,
She could float.
She became light.
Lighter than ever.
Than ever before.
She became light.
Light, like a feather.
She became blissful.
Blissful with love.
She dropped her fear.
She left it back there.
Back there,
The weight is gone.
All of the weight.

This weight, she carried.
It weighed her down.
She put all of it down.
She let it all go.
She became light.
Light, like a feather.
She became free.
Free, like a bird.
She can float.
She can fly.
She can be anything she wants.
She is light now.
Lighter,
Than ever.

My Intuitive Gift

The more time I spend alone,
The more intuitive I become.
Intuition is my gift.
My gift that I give.
I have this intuition.
This intuition in me.
This intuition is strong.
This intuition is my gift.
My gift that I give.
I give to the world.
My gift that I found.
That I found in my love.
Inside of my love.
My love for myself.
This is my gift.
My gift that I give.
My intuition.
This feeling.
This deep knowing.
My intuitive guide.
That guides me to the light.
The light for me.
My light.
My light that I found.
This light in me.
My light.
My gift.
My intuition.
All of this,
Inside of me.

I found it.
I embrace it.
I will cherish it,
And care for it.
Protect it.
Nurture it.
My intuition.
My intuitive self.
My gift that I give.
My gift that I found.
Found in my love.

Thank You

The people who are there.
Standing by your side.
Standing by your side,
During the darkness.
Standing by your side,
At the end of your journey.
The people who are there.
They are the people,
You least expect...
Standing by your side,
Cheering you on.
They are not the ones you ever imagined.
Imagined would be standing.
Standing by you.
They are not the ones you pictured in your mind.
Supporting you.
It is never who you think.
People will surprise you.
People will leave,
And never return.
The ones you thought,
Would be there giving you support.
People will surprise you.
They will surprise you.
People will shock you.
People will disappoint you.
People change,
And that's okay.
It is never the people.
The people you think.

It is usually the people,
Who are waiting in the wings.
It is usually the people,
That are not there every day.
People will surprise you.
People will lift you.
People will love you.
People will support you.
It is those people,
Standing at the end.
These are my people.
I am thankful.
I am thankful I found you.
Thank you,
For your endless support.
Thank you for loving me.
Loving me,
Unconditionally.
Thank you for being here.
Thank you for letting me be.
Thank you again,
For supporting me.

No Matter What

She found her flaws.
She found her weaknesses.
She found her downsides.
She found her shadow side.
She embraced all of these,
As she became vulnerable.
Vulnerable with herself.
She discovered her needs,
And started putting herself first.
She finally saw.
Saw herself.
Saw herself fully.
She embraced herself.
Flaws and all.
She found her love.
Love for herself.
Even her flaws.
Instead of picking herself apart...
She took each flaw,
And held it close.
She learned to love each part of herself.
Even those hard parts,
That were so hard to see.
She stopped pulling herself apart.
She stopped ripping herself to shreds.
She stopped punishing herself,
She finally looked at her reflection with love.
"I love you."
She said.
"No matter what.

Unconditionally,
Through and through."
Her flaws and all.
Her mistakes and quirks.
Her stubborn ways.
Her rebellious side.
Her careless side.
Her emotional side.
Her sensitive side.
She needed to learn to love herself,
In ways that she never was loved before.
"I love you,
No matter what."
This is what she needed,
From day one.
She started to believe,
In her worth again.
She felt her worth,
As she felt her love.
Her unconditional love,
No matter what.
"No matter what you do.
No matter where you go.
No matter what you say.
No matter what,
My love is there.
My love for you,
Unconditionally."

This Wildflower

Be careful who you spend time with.
Be careful who you exchange energy with.
This is who you become.
You will become this.
Be careful with your space.
This space that you give.
This space that you take from.
Be careful with your exchange.
Any exchange is energy.
An energy exchange.
This exchange is what you become.
The world you live in,
Is what you will be.
The world you live in,
Is what you see.
The world you live in.
This becomes your world.
Choose wisely.
The energy around you,
Is what you become.
The energy around you,
Is who you will be.
Your energy is important.
Be careful with it.
Be careful with your energy.
Protect it.
This is who you are.
Your energy.
Your beliefs.
What you accept.

Who you become.
Your energy is important.
Your community is too.
Where do you belong?
Where do you fit?
Maybe you don't fit anywhere.
Maybe your world is everywhere.
Maybe you belong in nature.
Maybe you belong in a field.
A field full of wildflowers.
Maybe you belong by the water.
Maybe you belong, grounding yourself.
Maybe you belong with the trees.
Maybe you belong where the wildflowers grow.
Maybe you belong at the beach.
Maybe you belong, connecting with the earth.
Maybe you belong sitting under the sun.
Maybe you belong in the moonlight.
Maybe you belong with the stars.
Maybe you belong where the wildflowers are.
Maybe because,
That is what you are.
This beautiful, radiant wildflower.
This wildflower that grows.
Grows anywhere and everywhere.
Anywhere the wind blows.
This beautiful, blissful wildflower.
This wildflower is free.
This wildflower has a spirit.
This spirit that is free.
This free-spirited wildflower,
That blooms wherever she ends up.

She blooms with whatever storm that comes.
The storms that come to take her down.
These storms come to destroy her.
This beautiful wildflower that she is.
But no matter the rain and the wind.
No matter the storms that arise.
No matter the earth-shattering hurricanes.
This wildflower remains.
This beautiful, peaceful wildflower.
This wildflower is her.
This wildflower will grow,
No matter what.
This wildflower is beautiful,
No matter what.
This wildflower that blooms anywhere.
And everywhere,
She will bloom.
She will bloom in the sun.
She will bloom with the trees.
She will bloom with the breeze.
She will bloom with the storms.
No matter what,
This wildflower remains.
This wildflower is strong.
This wildflower is beautiful.
This wildflower glows.
This wildflower is free.
This wildflower is her.

Freedom

The freedom to choose.
The freedom to be.
The freedom to let go.
Let go of it all.
Letting go brings freedom.
A freedom she never knew.
A freedom of light.
A freedom of love.
This freedom,
She found.
Found for herself.
This freedom is found.
Found in her heart.
This freedom is found,
Inside of stillness.
This freedom,
Her soul.
Her soul is radiating.
Radiating a vibration.
A vibration she's never felt.
This vibration of love.
Breathe in.
Breathe out.
This vibration.
Wait just a moment.
Enjoy this sensation.
This sensation of love.
This love is vibrating out.
Out to the world.
This vibration she knows.
She knows it as love.

Love that she never knew existed.
Existed in her.
She never knew it was there.
Looking for it externally,
Everywhere.
This love,
This light.
This is freedom.
This freedom that came,
When she chose herself.
Nothing else matters,
Feel the pain.
Shrug off the small things,
Keep moving forward.
She wouldn't know this light,
If it wasn't for the darkness.
Ending this suffering.
This suffering she knew.
Detaching from her ego,
She has released it.
Detaching from everything,
As suffering is removed.
If they don't accept her,
That is okay.
If they don't choose her,
She will choose herself.
Detaching from it all,
Brought her here.
Here to herself.
Here to her heart.
Here to her love.
This love for herself.

Thank you.
Sending you love.

I dedicate this book to my sister, as we walk this journey together, side by side.